Stitch in Bloom

Stitch in Bloom

Botanical-inspired embroidery projects for you and your home

Hardie Grant
BOOKS

Photography by Matt Russell

LORA AVEDIAN

Chain Stitch
Lazy Daisy
Satin Stitch
Stem Stitch

Contents

Introduction

This book takes a new look at the versatility of a traditional embroidery technique called couching (also known as cording). I first realised that this was a technique I was drawn to when studying for my master's degree in mixed media textiles. We were tasked with a stitch project, taking a list of embroidery stitches which we had to research and then interpret in our own way. This project led me to look further into these techniques, and I discovered that couched Russia braid is frequently used as embellishment for folk costume around the world. Looking to my family history for inspiration, I found the same technique used on a treasured antique textile piece that my father owned and which had been passed down from his Armenian ancestors. This wall hanging has swirling lines of cord that create a playful and tactile pattern on the surface of the fabric.

This way of drawing, using a single line of embroidery, seemed to be the perfect means for me to translate my designs into stitch. While creating samples with different materials, I realised that it's possible to get a really broad variety of outcomes with this one simple technique. As a mixed media textile designer, I love to use this embroidery stitch in combination with different embellishment techniques, such as appliqué, which is something I touch on in a couple of the projects, but for me this book is a celebration of the simplicity and versatility of couching.

Each project in this book is inspired by British flowers, from those found growing in the wild to those tended in everyday gardens. Before we get stuck in, I will guide you through everything you need to know, from tools and materials through to the basic stitches and how to create your own designs. I hope you take inspiration from my designs and work with them in a way that suits your materials and colour palette.

What Is Couching?

Couching is the main embroidery stitch we will be working with throughout this book. This is an embroidery technique where single or multiple threads, cord, yarn or any strip of material – referred to throughout the book as base yarns – are attached or anchored to the surface of the fabric using small regular stitches – called top threads. These stitches run across the chosen material, either from side to side or down the centre, depending on what material is used and the overall effect you want to achieve. Traditionally this technique is often seen in gold work embroidery and can be used in quantity and close together to fill a space, or simply to follow a single line of a pattern.

The reason I love working with this stitch is its versatility. You can use the technique with so many materials, and each one will produce a different finish. Variations, such as the thickness of your couched material compared to the background material you are working on and how far apart or ordered your stitches are, can completely change the outcome of your design. In the project section I will show you some of my favourite materials to use and how I use them in different contexts with varying weights of fabric.

How To Use This Book

I hope that the projects in this book will provide something for everyone, whether you have just started stitching or are an accomplished embroiderer. The projects have been designed to show you the variety of ways the technique of couching can be used.

Each project has step-by-step instructions, and there are templates of each flower and leaf motif. You may want to recreate the projects exactly as they are shown, but I would also encourage you to use the book as inspiration to create your own original work or to take the embroidery designs to use in different contexts. For example, you could adapt the Fallen Leaves Table Runner on page 124 by swapping the leaf motifs for flower motifs from other projects.

Before attempting the projects, please take a look at the Getting Started section, which begins on page 14, for inspiration on colour palettes, motifs and materials, and advice on how to design your own patterns and transfer them to your fabric. Then, use the skills you have learned and apply them to the designs in this book. One of the simplest to start with is the Tulip Scarf on page 94, which uses a single stitch in a single line to create the flower design, making this ideal for someone who is new to embroidery. For someone more confident or looking to push themselves, there are more challenging decorative techniques in more advanced projects like the Foxglove Wall Hanging on page 138, which uses a combination of techniques.

All in all, there are not many stitches to learn, but there are lots of variations. The stitch index on pages 29–39 is a great source of reference, reminding you of the basics of each stitch. I would recommend practising the stitches with samples of the materials (the base yarn and top thread) you want to use for the project before you start. If you do not have exactly the same materials as I have used, the idea is that you will be able to use the techniques to work with any materials, and hopefully it will inspire you to think a bit differently about your embroidery and create your own individual pieces.

Although I encourage you to experiment, I have provided templates for the motifs in all of the projects, which you can find at the back of the book on pages 148–151. The templates have been placed at varying scales, and will need to be increased to 100 per cent when scanned or traced and printed out.

Getting Started

Finding Inspiration

Two of my favourite places to find inspiration for my embroideries are antique textiles fairs or second-hand markets. Car boot sales (trunk sales) are also one of my first ports of call to seek out odd things that could be inspiring – this could be anything from glass buttons to photographs or a ceramic vase. I collect objects that spark my imagination, and when you are designing your own work, I suggest you look at the objects that you own as a starting point. It could be the colours, the shape or the texture of an object or image that inspires you, perhaps taking one small detail to recreate as an embroidery.

I am an avid collector of books, especially botanical books and sewing books. I always look for these in second-hand shops and I keep them for inspiration. Searching on the internet and social media for images has become a huge part of my research, but nothing beats holding physical objects that have a history attached to them.

Museums and galleries are always a great place to start if you need to kickstart the design process. I really enjoy going to the glass and ceramics section of the Victoria and Albert Museum in London, as I often find permanent exhibitions of historical objects to be even more interesting than the fashion and textiles section.

Nature also has a huge influence on my work, and without wanting to sound clichéd, I have always felt the inspiration you can find in nature is never-ending. If I do not have time to sit and draw from life, I take quick photographs on my phone wherever I see a flower I like. I find a lot of the best ones growing in the front gardens I pass while walking around my local area in south-west London. Because my garden isn't a floral paradise, I often look at the roses and dahlias growing outside my neighbours' gardens. If you live in an urban space and don't have a garden, keep your eyes peeled for wildflowers pushing up between cracks of concrete. I often see tall hollyhocks or wild poppies springing next to gates, fences or brick walls. Cut flowers or houseplants are another way of finding inspiration to draw from. As well as buying cut flowers from the supermarket, try visiting your local florist as they often stock flowers that are far more exciting or exotic. I sometimes go to my local flower market to see what is in season or seek out local growers. The joy of working with cut flowers is that you can create compositions with them by laying them out on your table or arranging them in a vase so you can draw from them in real life.

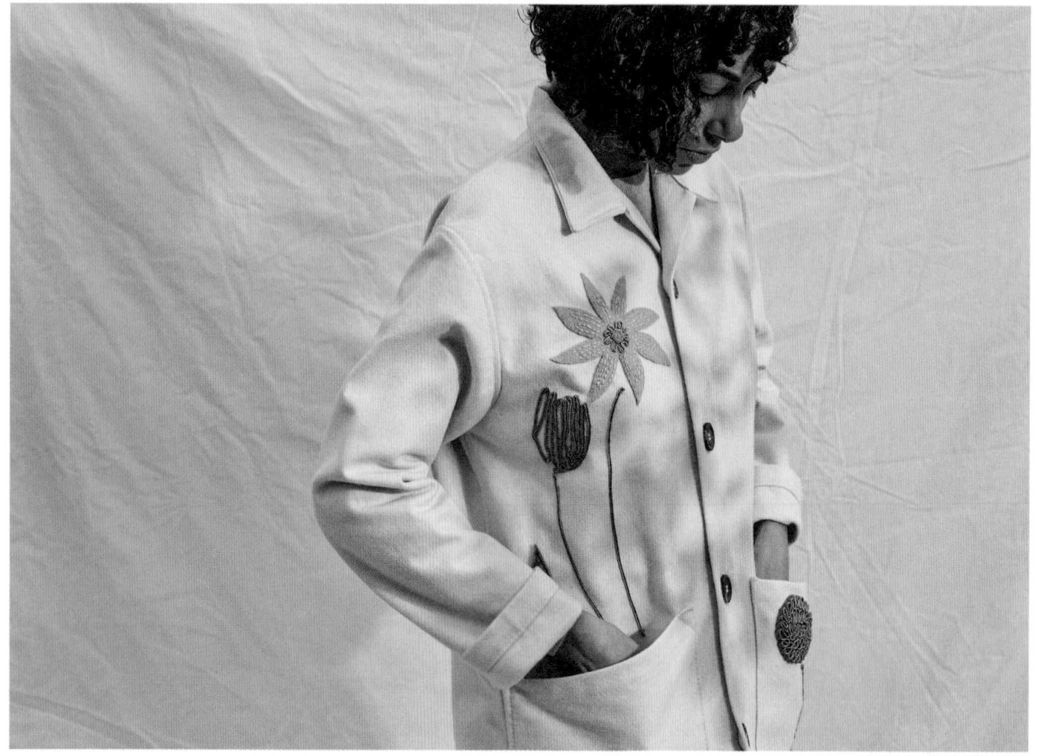

Working With Colour

When deciding on my colour palette for a project, I either work with materials I already have or source specific things in the right colours. For inspiration I often watch movies or look at photography and classical paintings, taking note of their colour schemes. I also have a collection of postcards from exhibitions I have visited over the years and this is always a good place to look for colour.

Putting a basic colour palette together on a piece of paper is a great way to start designing, even if that is with a combination of objects and materials. I often find objects such as small stones, leaves or tiny shells in colours I'm drawn to and stick them into my sketchbook, alongside small pieces of wool, ribbon or fabric I want to use in the project. Alternatively, you can paint a square of colour on white paper or find a scrap of coloured paper that is just right. Once you have your colours, try to source materials which match to them or, even better, dye them yourself if you have the time and skill.

If you are so inclined, spend time to develop your own colour palette. Collect a variety of materials so that you always have a good range of inspiration to work with for your projects. If you are not sure what to look for, find objects you are attracted to and work out a colour palette from those, such as a photograph that you like or a piece of ripening fruit. In my work I use variations on the same colour palette which I developed when studying for my master's degree. This reflects my research into my Armenian heritage, looking at stills from the cult Armenian movie *The Color of Pomegranates*, and ceramics, antique textiles and paintings I have found. If you are someone who enjoys working with colour, try making a sketchbook purely to explore colour and use this as a place to develop combinations which you can look back at and reference in future.

rmanent Yellow Deep

Tools

Over time you can invest in and build up a good collection of tools, but for me having a sharp pair of scissors, an embroidery hoop and some new needles is always a good foundation for starting a project. I would put particular emphasis on the new needles because for years I mistakenly used ones that I found in old sewing kits, but after working commercially as an embroiderer I realised how important it is to change your needles regularly. A blunt needle can be much harder to put through your fabric, as well as possibly causing damage to your material by catching the fibres. When working with something like a fine silk, you should make sure you have a really sharp needle.

You do not need to have all of these things (listed opposite) to start your work, and if you are new to this craft, I would encourage you to use equivalents that are easily accessible to you (for example, rather than investing in a lightbox, you can use daylight through a window). The idea is to give you options and you can choose which method works best for you. Sometimes you do just have to buy new things, but you may find you already have a lot of the material that's needed at the back of a desk drawer!

Mixture of hand embroidery needles (sizes 3–9)

The size of needle you use depends on the thickness of the sewing thread (top thread) you are using. Embroidery needles tend to be thin with a long, thin 'eye' for threading thicker embroidery thread (floss) through (you can flatten the thread to fit through the eye). It would also be useful to have a larger needle with an eye which can take a ribbon, strip of fabric or a length of yarn in case you want to hide the ends of your material in the fabric – this is often called a tapestry needle, which range from size 13 to 26.

Above

Your basic toolkit should include large hand sewing 'sharps' needles or 'darner' needles, dressmaking pins, sharp fabric scissors (small and large), PVA glue, paper or a sketchbook, embroidery hoops and a metal thimble. You might also need fabric pens, tailor's chalk, a lightbox, masking tape and tracing paper to transfer your designs.

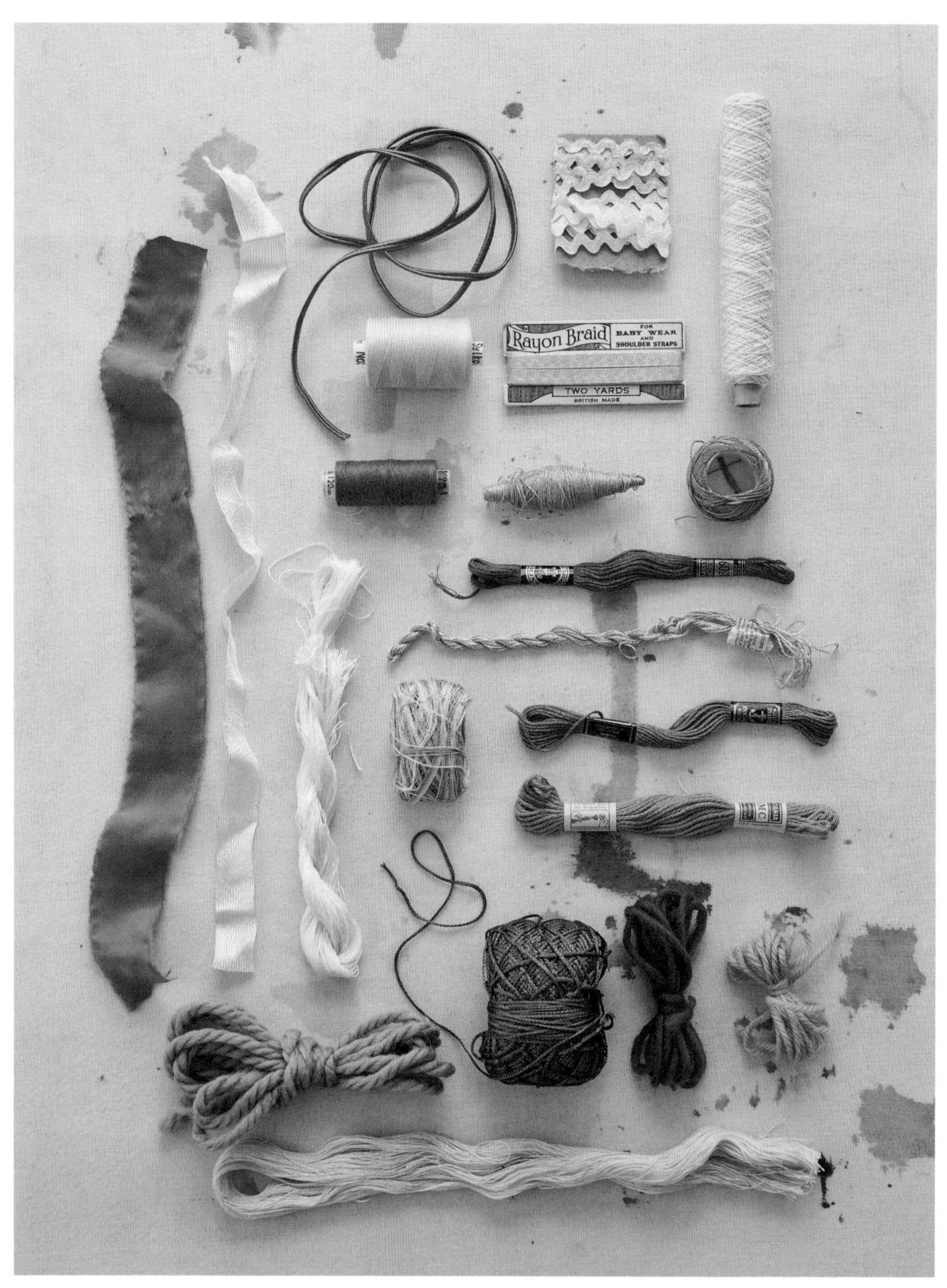

Above

Choose from a variety of top threads, including cotton embroidery thread (floss); twisted silk embroidery thread; cotton or polyester sewing threads; quilting or sashiko hand sewing threads; and linen embroidery threads. For base yarns, you can use ribbon, strips of fabric, Russia braid, embroidery thread, woollen yarn, ric-rac, raffia or paper yarn or any kind of braid, cord or rope.

Threads And Fabrics

One of the things I love about couching is that it can have such a varied array of finishes depending on the material you use. The effect of each material's weight, size, softness, flexibility and base fabric (the item you are embroidering on to) can change the outcome of the embellishment entirely.

When designing the projects for this book, I really wanted to emphasise how you can repurpose materials already in your home without needing to buy new. The beauty of this technique is that you can use strips of any material or small lengths of yarn or threads that you have left over from other craft projects. You can bundle up scraps of thread that you have cut, tear up an item of clothing you haven't worn in years or even use household string. I have boxes full of scraps because I can't bear to throw them into landfill, so I used this book as an opportunity to use a lot of the materials I already had around me. I encourage you to do the same. Second-hand markets are also a great opportunity to find materials that you can use in your work. Look out for old sewing boxes in charity shops and thrift stores, as these are often where I find some of my best embroidery threads and small scraps of ribbon or yarn. On lucky days I have found rolls of antique Russia braid or ribbon at markets or fairs, and these are even more special because I know I only have a limited amount of it and have to plan my designs thoughtfully. The quality of these vintage materials is often better than modern versions too.

To the left is a selection of materials that work well with couching. Once you have mastered the basic stitches, I encourage you to experiment so you can see the huge possibilities of this stitch.

Stitch Index

Here you have instructions for each of the stitches I have used in this book – use this as an index which you can refer back to whenever you need to.

The basic couching stitch and the back stitch are the most important ones to learn, and once you feel confident with those two techniques, it is just a case of choosing which materials you would like to work with. My hope is that this gives you the basis on which to experiment with materials you already have at home.

Before beginning a project, I recommend trying a small sample using your chosen materials and techniques so you can see what the finished result will look like. It is also really useful to have a sampler to reference for future projects.

Every stitch technique has drawn illustrations, and overleaf you can see examples of the different materials you can use with each. Different materials produce a particular finished look to your work, but as well as there being variations in materials, there are many variations of stitches.

The main stitches used in this book are:

Basic couching stitch
Back stitch
Stab stitch
Blanket stitch
Running stitch
French knot
Whip stitch

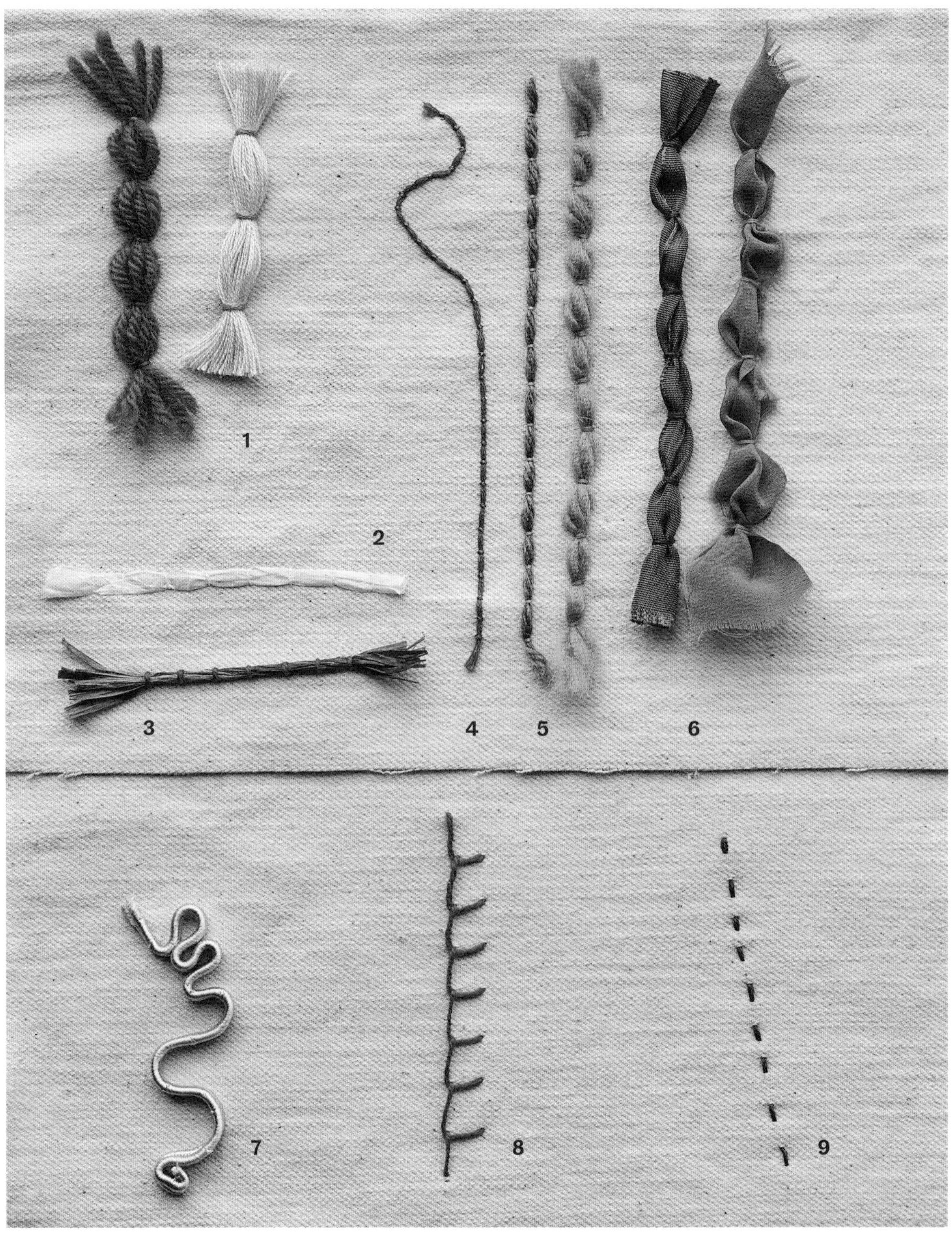

Basic couching stitch in multiple wool and cotton threads **(1)**; Bamboo tape **(2)**; Natural raffia **(3)**; Embroidery thread (floss) **(4)**; Standard and chunky wool yarn **(5)**; Ribbon and silk crepe **(6)**; Stab stitch **(7)**; Blanket stitch **(8)**; Running stitch **(9)**

Back stitch couching in silk, woven ribbon and satin ribbon **(10)**; Russia braid **(11)**; Ric-rac **(12)**; Bamboo tape **(13)**; French knots **(14)**; Whip stitch **(15)**

BASIC COUCHING STITCH

This is the main stitch used throughout the projects. I am describing how to stitch down a length of embroidery thread (floss) or thin wool yarn.

1. Thread your needle with embroidery thread (floss) and knot at one end.
2. Place your base yarn on your fabric and pin it in place along your design.
3. Put your needle into your fabric from the back of your material, coming through on the left side of your base yarn.
4. Pull your needle and thread through to the front and take it directly over to the opposite side of your base yarn in a straight line and down into the fabric very close to where you came out, roughly 1 mm (1⁄16 in) away **(Fig. 1)**.
5. Do a couple of the stitches like this in the same place to start with, then move on to your next stitch 1 cm (½ in) along from your first one, again coming up on the left side of your base yarn, and going back down again on the right of your base yarn. You can make your stitches closer together and experiment with the frequency of them.
6. Use your thumb of your non-dominant hand to hold and guide your base yarn as you continue along your line or use pins to keep your base yarn in place.

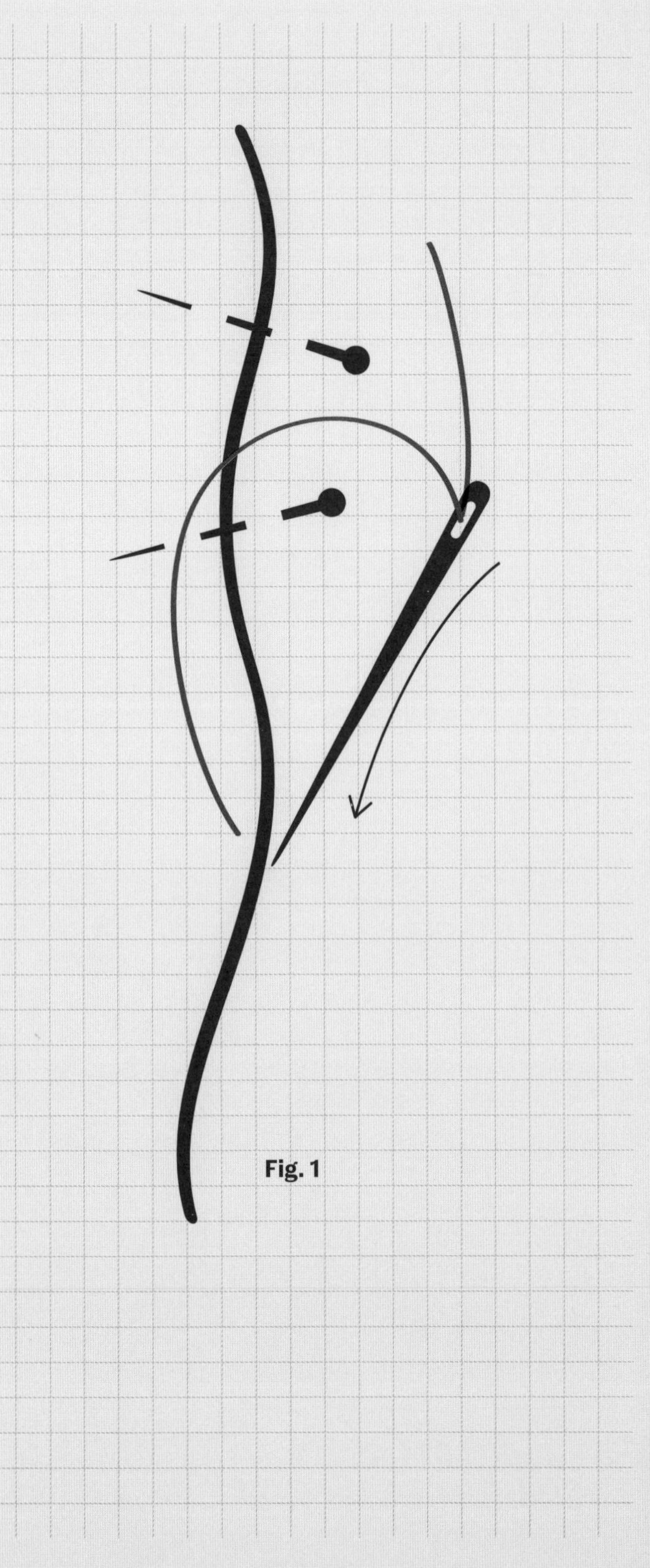

Fig. 1

BACK STITCH

For this example of the back stitch I am using braid, but the instructions work for all of the other materials listed in the stitch variations on **page 31**.

1. Finish off the end of your braid with glue and fold it under itself to hide the end. Thread your needle with a double thread that matches the colour of your braid and knot the ends of the threads together. Pin down your braid in a few places along your drawn line. Come up through the back of your fabric at the end of your braid, with your starting point a stitch length (2–3 mm/⅛ in) along from the end of the braid **(Fig. 1)**. This should be through the end which you have glued and folded, and you should be working down the centre of your braid.

2. Pull your thread through and put the needle back down behind where you first came up so you are working back towards the beginning of your braid **(Fig. 2)**. Do a second stitch in this exact same place to start with, to secure it in place.

3. For the next stitch, come up from the back of your fabric roughly 5 mm (¼ in) along from your last stitch **(Fig. 3)**.

4. Put your needle down behind where you came up **(Fig. 4)**, as if you are going towards the end of your braid, doing a stitch about 1–2 mm (1⁄16 in) in size. Continue going forward and looping back along your braid every 5 mm (¼ in). Guide your braid with your thumb as you go, or pin it down along your design.

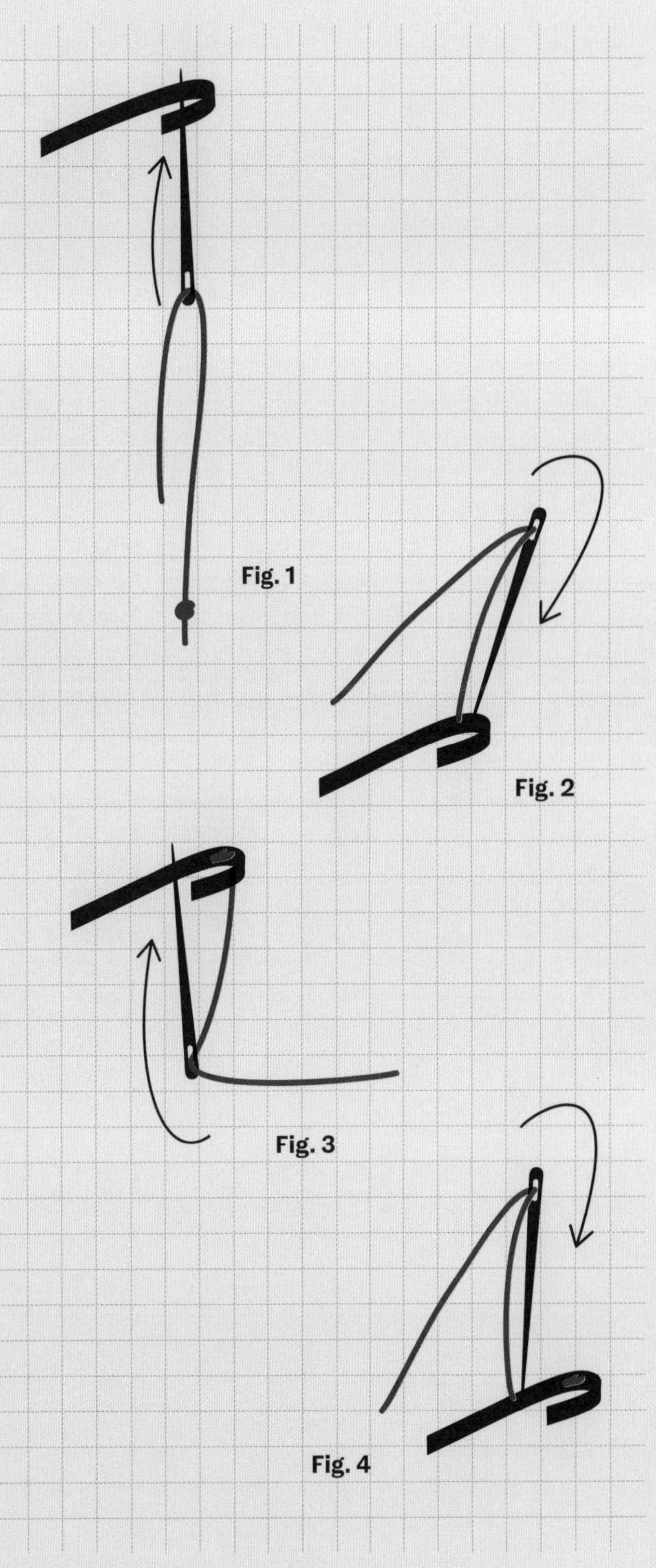

STAB STITCH

Stab stitch is used for sewing down Russia braid on its side. It gives a different quality of line, I prefer to use braid 4 mm (1⁄6 in) or wider for this technique.

1. Seal the end of your braid with a dab of glue. Thread your needle up with a double length of sewing thread and knot the ends together.

2. Holding the braid on it's side between your thumb and index finger, work your needle through the side of the braid instead of down the centre **(Fig. 1)**. Coming up from underneath, put your needle straight through the fabric into the side of the braid and pull your thread all the way through.

3. Come back down into the braid in almost exactly the same place as you came out, **(Fig. 2)** going all the way through the side of the braid again. This is so your stitch is not seen – you should have a very small dot of thread visible on the top of your braid. To make it even less visible, try to match your top thread to your braid.

This can also be couched down from the back of your fabric, but I find that does not always work as well unless you are covering the area quite densely with braid.

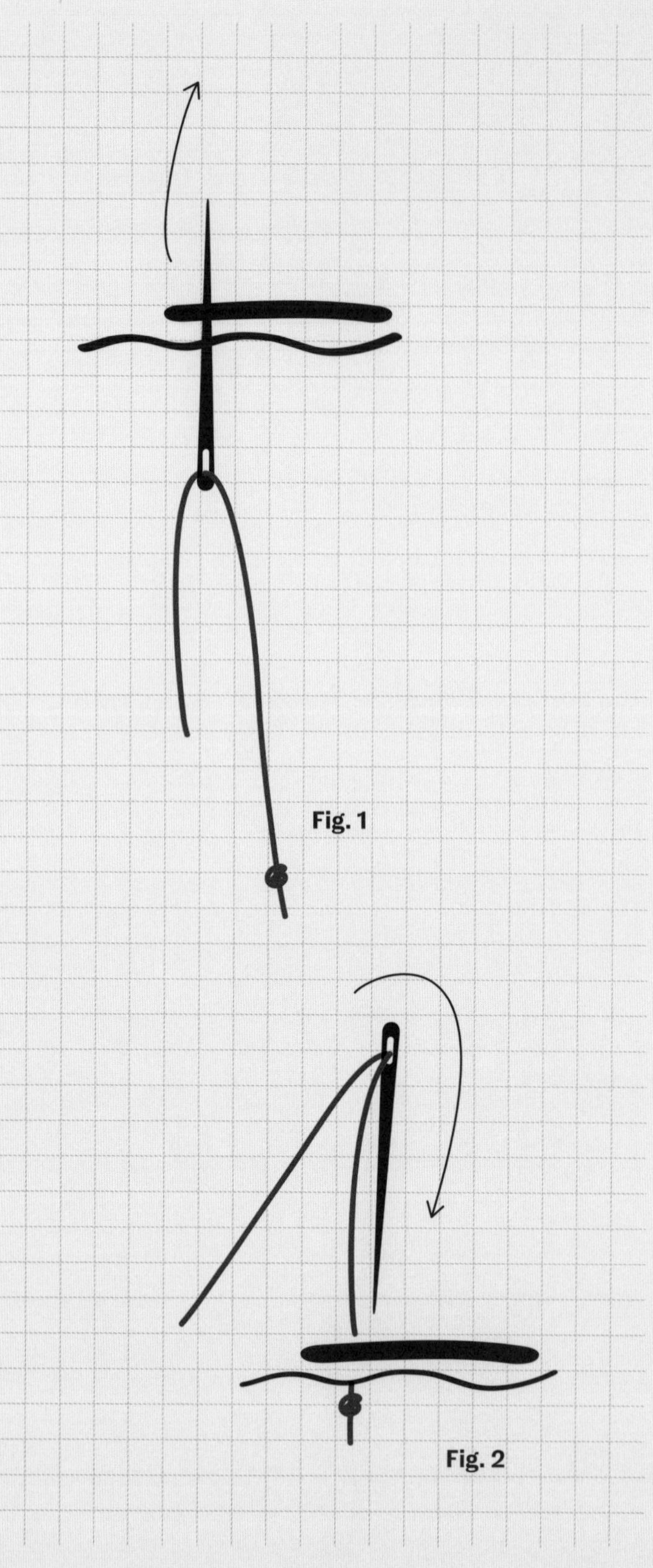

Fig. 1

Fig. 2

BLANKET STITCH

This stitch is a decorative way of couching down your yarn and creates a line along one side of your couched line, so think about which side you want this line to be in relation to your design. You can see an example of this used in the Rudbeckia Linen Curtain **on page 88**.

1. Thread your needle with your top thread and tie a knot in one end.
2. Start at the bottom of your length of base yarn by pulling your thread through from the back of your fabric on the right side of your base yarn.
3. Then put the needle back down into the fabric on the opposite side of the base yarn around 5 mm (¼ in) along, keeping a large loose loop rather than pulling it tight.
4. Now come back up from the back of the fabric on the right-hand side again opposite your last stitch point so you will be about 5 mm (¼ in) up from where you started **(Fig. 1)**. Put your needle through the loop you made, and pull the thread tight across your base yarn **(Fig. 2)**. Finish your line of stitching by sewing a few times in the same place and tying a small knot at the back of the fabric.

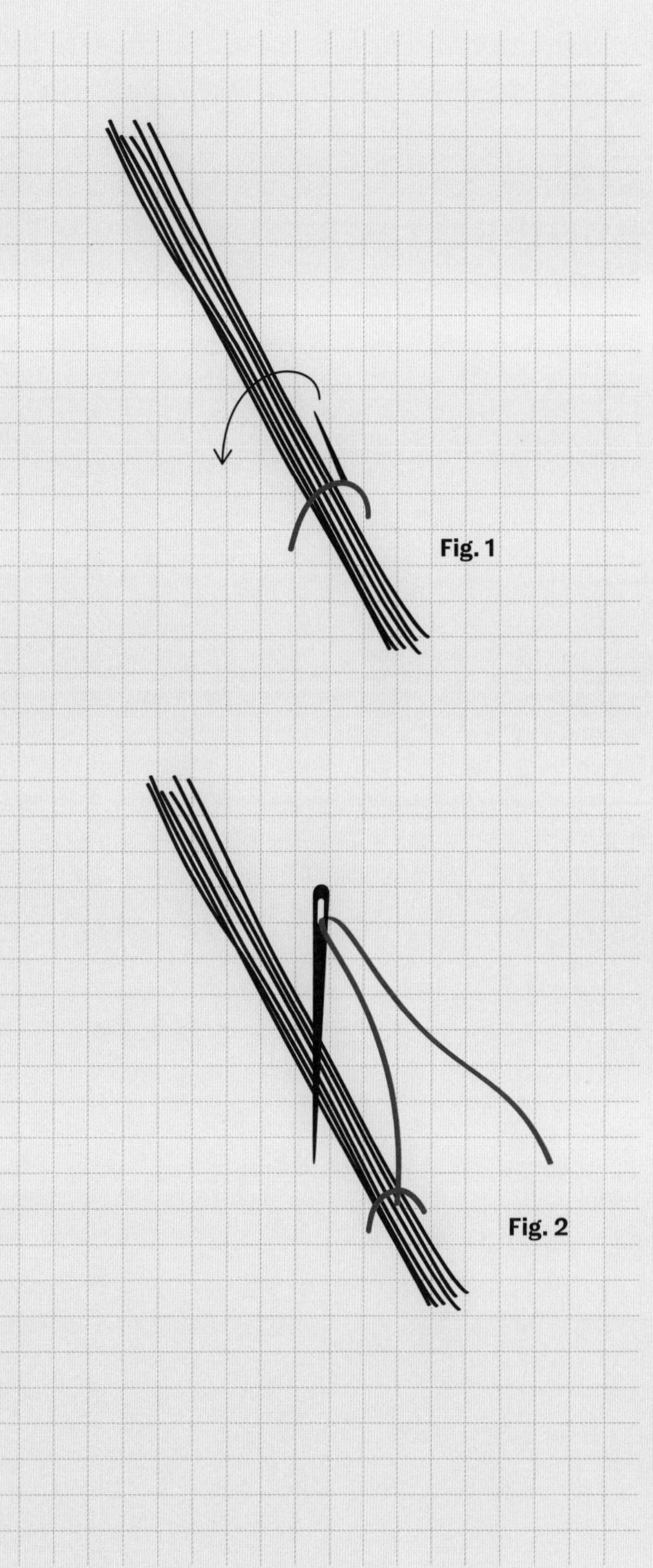

RUNNING STITCH

This is a simple stitch which is often used in hand quilting and works well with embroidery thread (floss). It can also be used as a decorative stitch. The length and distance between your stitches can vary with this technique, so you can use these instructions as a basic guide to work from.

1. Start by threading your needle and tying a knot in one end.
2. Bring your needle up through the fabric from the back to the front, pulling your thread all the way through.
3. Then put the needle back down again 3–4 mm (⅛ in) away from where you came out originally, going forward along your line.
4. Continue to do your next stitch in a straight line along from your last by coming up just beyond where your first stitch ended. The distance between your stitches and length of your stitches is up to you, but for this purposes keep them 1–2 mm (1⁄16 in) apart and roughly 3 mm (⅛ in) long **(Fig. 1)**.

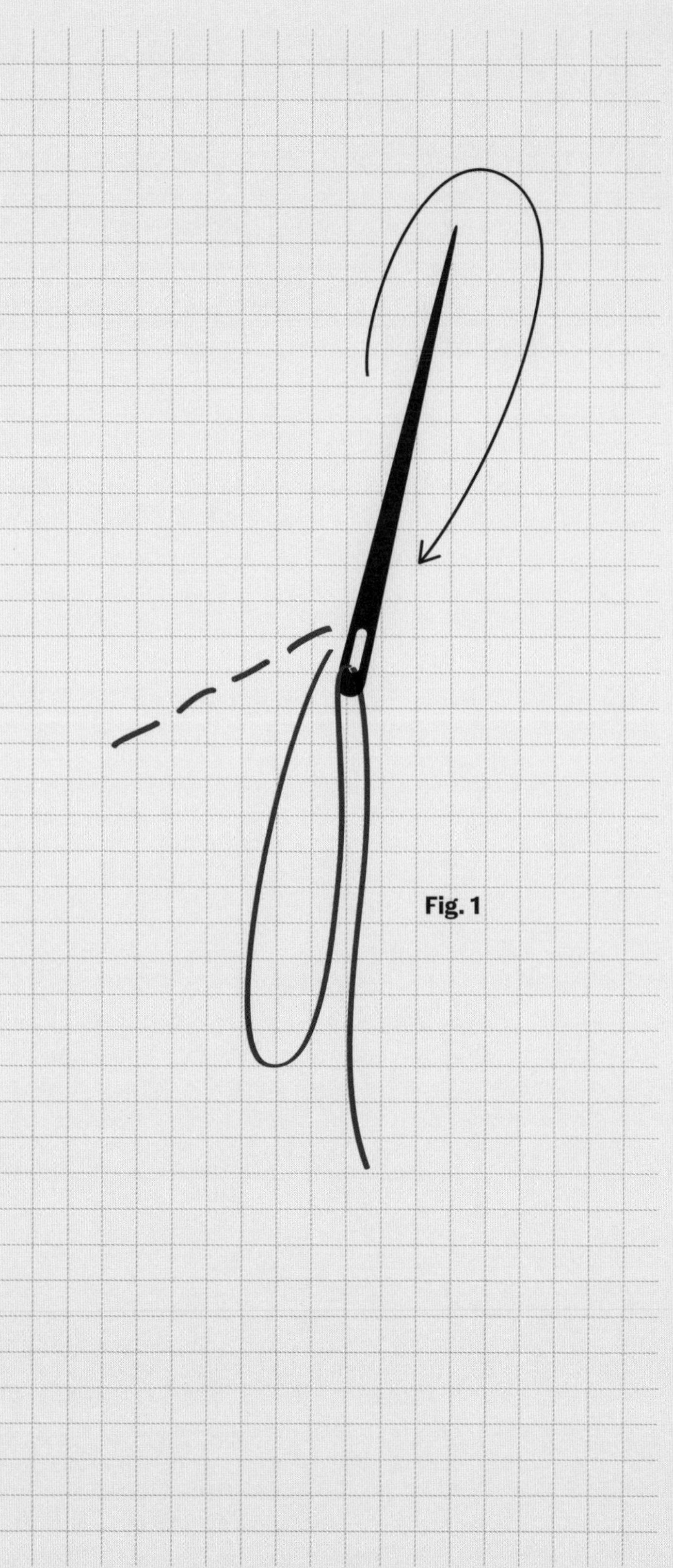

Fig. 1

FRENCH KNOT

A French knot is a really nice stitch to have in your repertoire as it works very well in the centre of flowers. You can make the knots larger or smaller depending on the material you use.

1. Thread your needle with a single length of embroidery thread (floss) and knot it at one end.
2. Push your needle into your fabric from the back. Pull the thread through until the knot meets the back of the fabric.
3. Using your non-dominant hand, hold your thread (floss) about 3 cm (1¼ in) away from where it came out of the fabric. Use that same hand to wrap the thread twice around the end of the needle.
4. Pull the thread fairly tight around the needle and put the point of your needle back down in the fabric right next to where it originally came out **(Fig. 1)**. Use your hand on your thread here to loosen the thread a little, making sure it is close to your fabric but doesn't slip off your needle. You should be able to move the needle through the loops easily.
5. Pull your thread all the way through your fabric loops **(Fig. 2)**, which should now be caught down securely, and form a little knot.

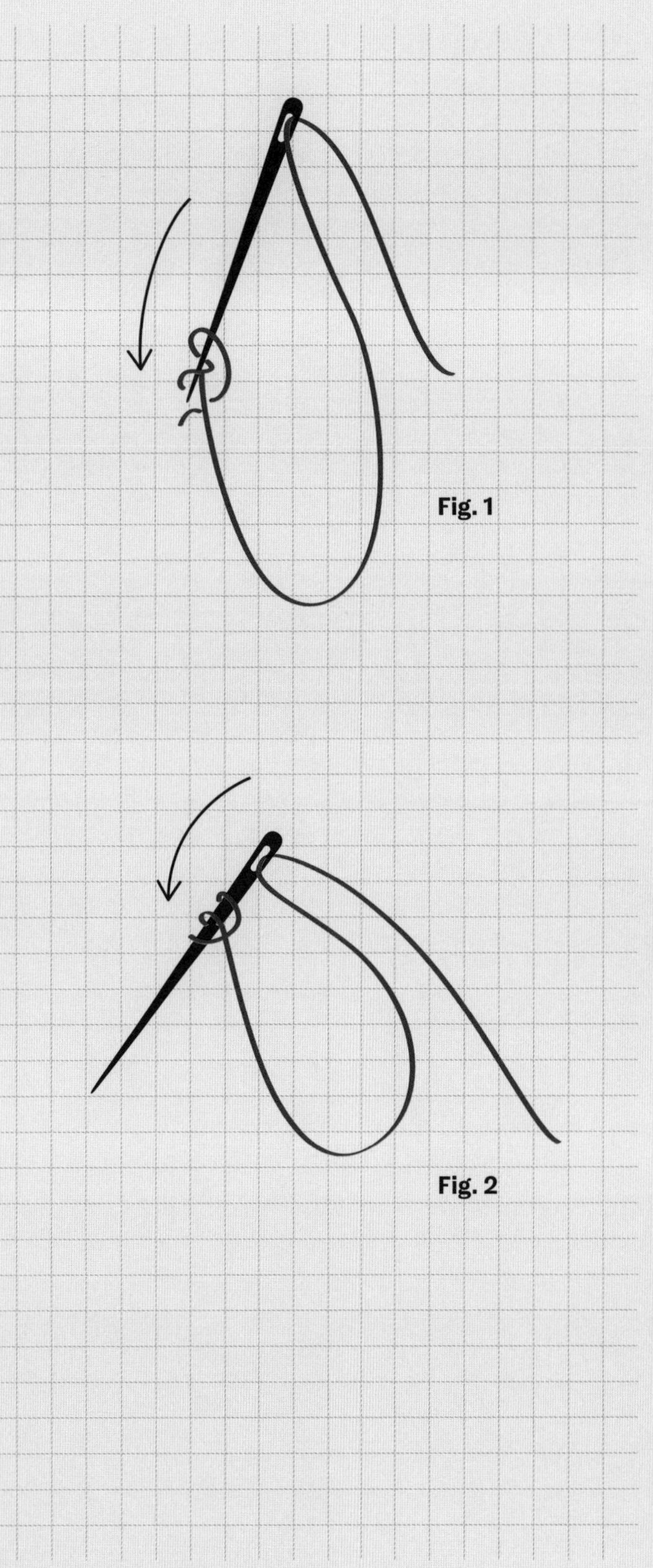

Fig. 1

Fig. 2

WHIP STITCH

Whip stitch is a sewing technique which can be used to bring two pieces of fabric together. It is also used in appliqué.

1. Thread your needle with a single or double length of thread – depending on the seam and material you're using. Knot the end of the thread.

2. If you are pulling two pieces of fabric together, pin these together before starting to sew. For the wall hanging or curtain lay them on a flat surface.

3. Start at one end of the gap by putting the needle 2 mm (⅛ in) inside one edge of the fabric **(Fig. 1)** and pull the thread all the way through, so the knot is in between the two pieces of fabric and will be hidden inside the seam.

4. Pass the needle and thread over the gap, and down about 2 mm (⅛ in) away from where the thread came out **(Fig. 2)**, just on the edge of where the fabric should be folded under, so you are working on a diagonal into the other piece of fabric.

5. Instead of pulling the needle all the way through the fabric right away, put the needle straight across into the side where you began, coming out of the fabric just on the edge **(Fig. 3)**. Make sure your tension is fairly loose - do not pull the edges together too tightly; they should just butt up to one another.

6. Continue as you did in step 4 until you have reached the top of the gap and the seam is closed.

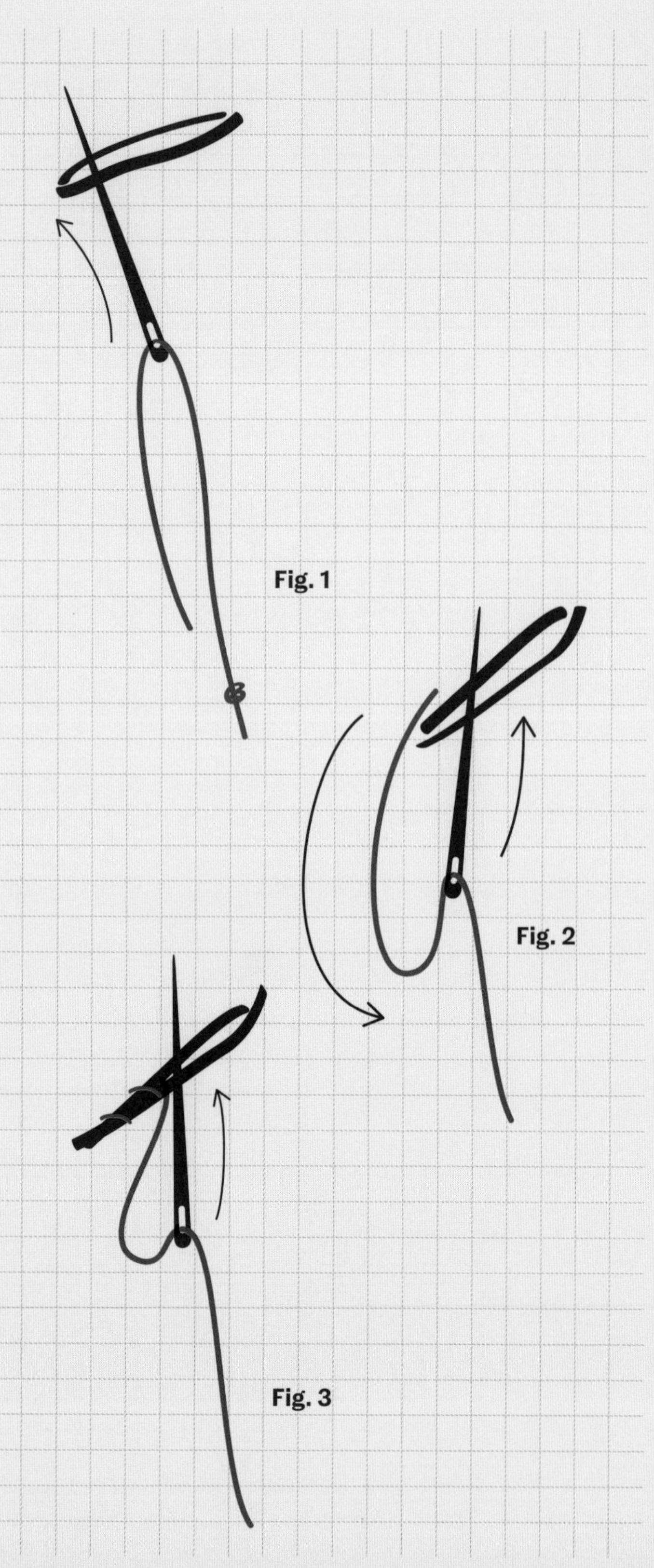

Other Ways To Use Embroidery Stitches

There are many more ways of using these stitches beyond a simple line drawing.

Clockwise from top right

Filling in space/shapes with materials
Creating pattern with stitch
Zigzag petals with silk
Loops of ribbon
Fringing and tassels
Zigzag petals with braid
Coiling around

Designing Your Pattern

A pattern can be designed in many different ways, from drawings you have done or photographs you have taken – I often use a combination of those things. Although drawing from life is the best thing to do, sometimes I just don't have the time to sit down and draw all the things I want to.

I find taking photographs to be a really useful way of collecting original inspiration. I try to work with the natural composition of how a flower grows, because this is usually more dynamic. More often than not I print out photographs and make a collage with them to create my own new composition. I have always loved working with collage, and I use it as a quick way to create designs. This could be done digitally by all means, but I like the physicality of cutting and pasting.

The nature of couching stitch is a continuous line, so I find it is best to simplify my drawings as much as I can by drawing over my flowers using a single line. The way you draw your design out can be dictated by the materials you are planning to use, and so can the kind of flower you are planning to design. If you want to fill a space or create a pattern with your stitches, it is worth drawing these things out on your fabric, so you have a guide to work along. See examples of variations on filling a leaf shape opposite.

If you are drawing from living flowers, try to draw without too much detail and keep your pen on the page; practise doing quick single-line drawings without looking down at your paper if you can.

TIP

Leaves can be created in many ways – here are a few suggestions:

Filling the leaf with a cord, embroidery thread (floss) or wool.

Folded ribbon – if you use a wide ribbon and stitch it down using back stitch, you can fold and pin down the ribbon to create a leaf shape.

Appliqué – by cutting a solid block of colour from something like wool felt, you can just stitch it down as a solid shape or add detail by embroidering into it.

Transferring Your Pattern Onto Fabric

Once you have decided on your pattern, base yarn and top threads, you need to mark the design out on your fabric. There are a few ways to do this.

Tracing with a window or lightbox

If you are working with thin to medium-weight fabrics, like linen, cotton or silk, and on a small scale, you can put your drawing on a lightbox and trace over it with a fabric pen of your choice.

Before I got my lightbox, I used to tape up my drawings to a sunny window – this is the simplest way to do it but doesn't work so well if you are working with a large pattern or if you have a thick fabric. Using masking tape, tape your drawings to the window, then tape your fabric over the top of the drawing and trace with your chosen fabric pen. This works best on linen, cotton and lightweight materials.

When working on a large scale, I draw my designs freehand, stepping away regularly to check on the composition or make a to-scale template. I do this by drawing out my design on tracing paper or pieces of scrap paper, cutting them out and pinning them on the fabric to draw around. This gives you a basic idea of where the shapes will be placed on the material, and then you can add more detail freehand. I particularly like drawing on tracing paper to map out my work as you can see the material underneath clearly, and it helps me to visualise the design better.

Using a stencil

If you want to be precise about where your stitching lines are going, you can make a stencil from scrap paper or tracing paper by cutting out all of your lines with a craft knife and going over them with your chalk. I find this works best on wool and heavier, darker materials.

Tacking (basting)

Another way to map out your design if you are working on dark fabric or a large-scale project which might take some time to complete is to tack (baste) the outline using a big running stitch. This will last longer, and I find it gives me a clearer line to work along. This is best to use on larger shapes or lines rather than small details which would take a very long time to stitch out. Use a thread that is a different colour from your background fabric and embroidery so that you can pull it out when your embroidery is complete.

Setting Up Your Hoop

Using an embroidery hoop is important as it helps to keep the fabric you are working on flat and taut. This tension of the fabric is important with a couching stitch as it enables your materials to lie flat against one another. It also allows you to focus on holding your base yarn down with your thumb and guiding it along your pattern.

To hoop up your fabric, place the smaller inside hoop on your table and put your fabric over the top, with the area to be stitched in the centre of the hoop. Place the larger outer hoop over the inner hoop and fabric, loosening or tightening the screw as necessary so that the outer hoop fits on top easily and snugly. To tighten your fabric so it is like a drum, keep your hoop on the table and put one hand over your frame with your fingertips on the edges of the circle pushing down onto the table. Now go around the edges of the hoop with your other hand, gently pulling the fabric out so it is taut, then tighten the screw again to secure the fabric in place.

TIP

Wrapping both sides of your hoop with a thin cotton bias tape, ribbon or strip of plain cotton fabric can reduce the marks made on the material, and can help grip the fabric into the hoop when you are working with thin or delicate materials like silk organza.

Textile Care

I hope these pieces of work you create will be kept and enjoyed for a long time, and in order to do that you need to treat them with care and store them correctly.

I always recommend that your textile pieces are kept out of direct sunlight to stop the colours of the material fading. If they are not being kept on display, keep them in a dry and dark container, free of moths.

All hand embroidery can be delicate, and people often ask me if the basic couching stitch is appropriate to be used on garments or soft furnishings. The nature of the basic couching technique is that it is vulnerable to being caught by things and pulled out of place. That is why I have used backstitched braid and ribbon for most of the garments or more practical soft furnishings, such as the cushion. This version of couching is much more hardwearing and I often use it on my cushion designs, rather than the more decorative and delicate couched yarns and threads. Looser yarns work best on framed or hung artworks, and it helps to iron them on the back to fix them in place. Of course there are no guarantees, but I believe that if you start and finish your embroidery with strong stitches and secure your base yarn down at regular intervals, you should not have any problems.

If you have to clean your embroidery, carefully hand wash your pieces using lukewarm water, delicate liquid laundry detergent and with minimal aggravation. This comes with risks though, and I would avoid it if you can. I also always recommend washing the materials that you are working on before you start embroidering them if possible, especially linen or cotton, and allow for a small amount of fabric shrinkage. Ironing the back of linen or cotton fabric when damp is always best, and always iron your embroidery on the back too.

If you are unable to or unsure about hand washing the material because of its delicacy, you could simply dust it regularly, or go over it with a clean, damp cloth. Alternatively, seek out specialist dry cleaners, although I would not recommend this because of the environmental impact.

Projects

Barley Placemat

A brightly coloured placemat is a great way to dress your table and bring some colour to your mealtimes. I have kept this design simple and used Russia braid which is backstitched onto the fabric so it can be washed after a meal. The minimalism of this barley-stem design creates a subtle and chic frame around your place setting.

You will need

Template (see page 144)
Pencil, tailor's chalk or dissolvable fabric pencil
4 placemats — I used readymade linen ones, 53 × 37 cm (21 × 14½ in)
Base yarn: Russia braid in off white/cream, 3 mm (½ in) thick, approximately 105 cm (41½ in) per stem
PVA glue
Top thread: sewing thread to match the colour of the Russia braid
Cotton embroidery thread (floss) to match the colour of the Russia braid
Hand embroidery or sewing needle
Small embroidery hoop
Dressmaking pins
Small sharp scissors

1. Trace the template **(see page 144)** onto the fabric – I added two barley stems to each placemat, positioning one along each long edge of the mat. You can draw over the pattern directly onto your fabric by copying the drawing onto paper and using a lightbox or a window to trace the drawing through onto the fabric **(see page 43)**.
2. Fix the end of the Russia braid with some glue and just before it's dry, fold it under itself to hide the end and prevent it fraying.
3. Thread your needle (I used a double length of matching sewing thread for this) and knot the end.
4. Place the fabric in the embroidery hoop, starting at the bottom of the stem, and pin the braid in place along the line within your hoop.
5. Sew a few stitches into the folded end of the braid to secure it in place at the end of the stem.
6. Using back stitch **(see page 33)** work along the straight line of the stem **(Fig. 1)**, stitching every 1 cm (½ in) until you reach the bottom of the barley spikelets. At this point, fold the braid back on itself at an angle to follow the drawn line. Do the same when you get to each point and need to turn a corner **(Fig. 2)**.
7. When you have finished the spikelets, continue back down the stem **(Fig. 1)**, butting close to the first row and finishing level with the starting point.

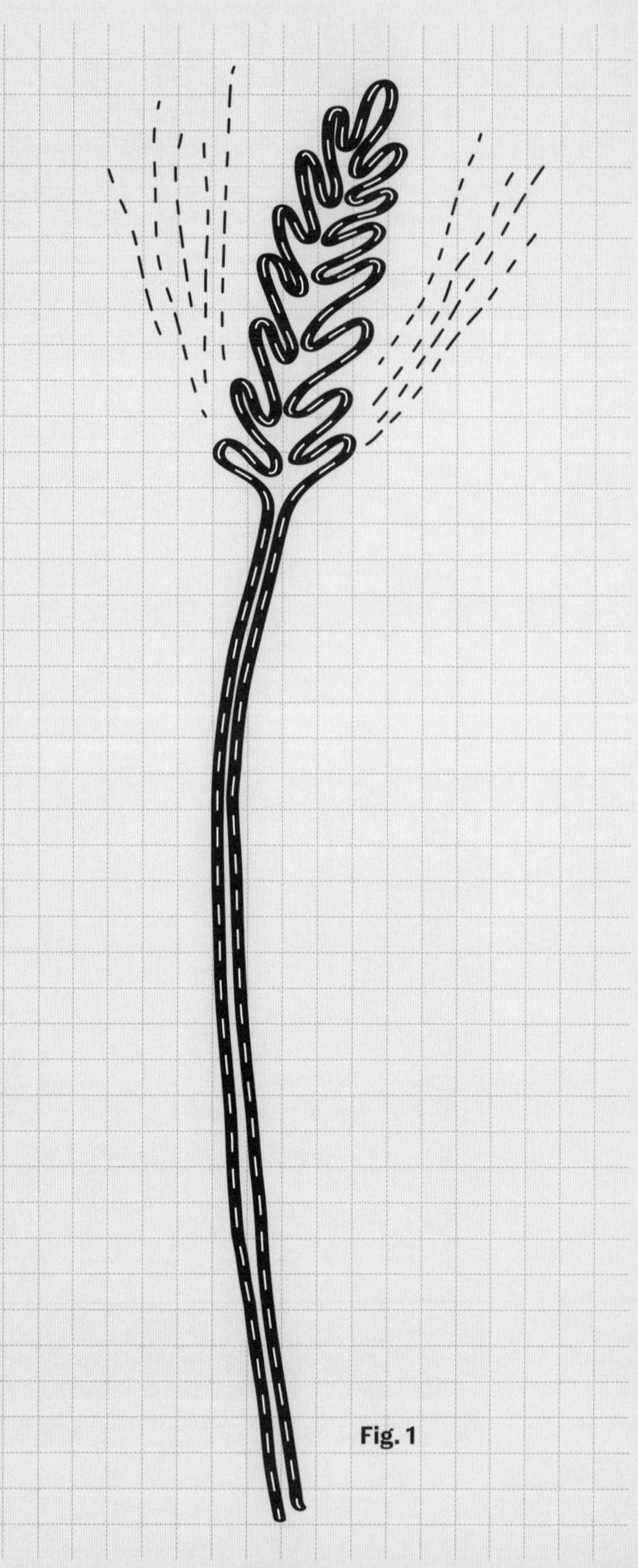

Fig. 1

8. Fasten off the thread on the underside of the placemat. Cut the braid, leaving enough to fold it back under itself. Fix the end (as in step 2) with some glue to stop it fraying.

9. I have added little whiskers to the barley stem to make it more realistic, using running stitch **(see page 36)** with a single strand of cotton embroidery thread (floss).

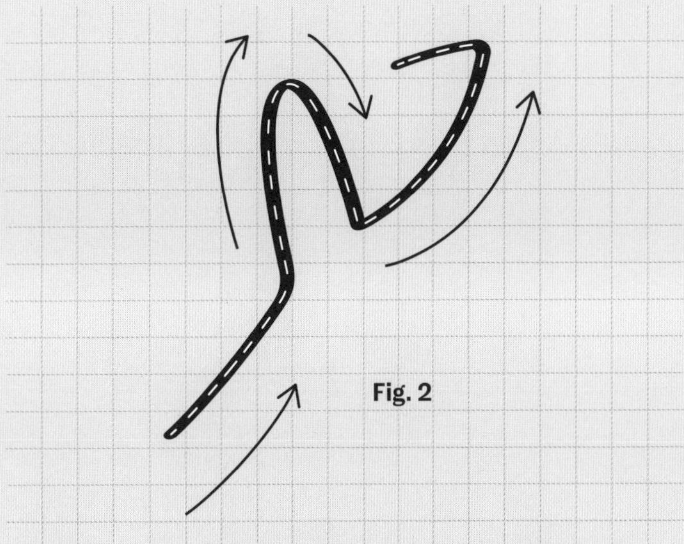

Fig. 2

Tulip Beret

Berets are the only hats I ever wear in the winter, and I think they are the perfect blank canvas to embroider. They are normally made from felted wool, so are really nice to sew into, and you can get them in so many different colours. The round shape gives a really interesting frame for a composition – it lends itself really well to big flower heads or curved stems, so for this one I have chosen the tulip, to match the scarf on page 94 but with the colours reversed.

You will need

Template (see page 60)
Tracing or scrap paper for template
Small sharp scissors
Dressmaking pins
Wool beret
Tailor's chalk (tends to work best on wool)
Tacking (basting) thread (optional)
Sharp large-eyed needle
Top thread: embroidery thread (floss) to match the colour of your beret
Base yarn: ball of woollen yarn to match the colour of the scarf on page 94

Note

You do not need a hoop for this because of the thickness of the wool fabric.

1. Draw your design on paper or copy the template **(Fig. 1)**. Make a stencil **(see page 43)**, cut it out and pin it in place on the beret. Use chalk to trace over the stencil. Or you can tack (baste) the outlines of the shapes first with large stitches **(see page 44)**.

2. Thread your needle with embroidery thread (floss) and knot at one end. I have used three strands of a six-strand thread skein and have not doubled my thread.

3. Start by pinning a small section of the base yarn along the chalk line, leaving a tail end overhanging the edge of the beret. Using basic couching stitch **(see page 32)**, start by making a couple of stitches in the same place to secure the base yarn. Follow your drawn lines with the base yarn, placing the stitches 1 cm (½ in) apart.

4. When you reach the top of the stem, fill the tulip head with the base yarn by zigzagging vertically along the petals, following the drawn lines **(Fig. 2)**.

5. Continue to fill the design, using one long length of wool. To finish off, go over your last stitch a couple of times. Then take the needle through to the inside of the beret and make a small knot at the back.

6. Trim all loose threads and the ends of the base yarn. Embroider the second tulip motif in the same way.

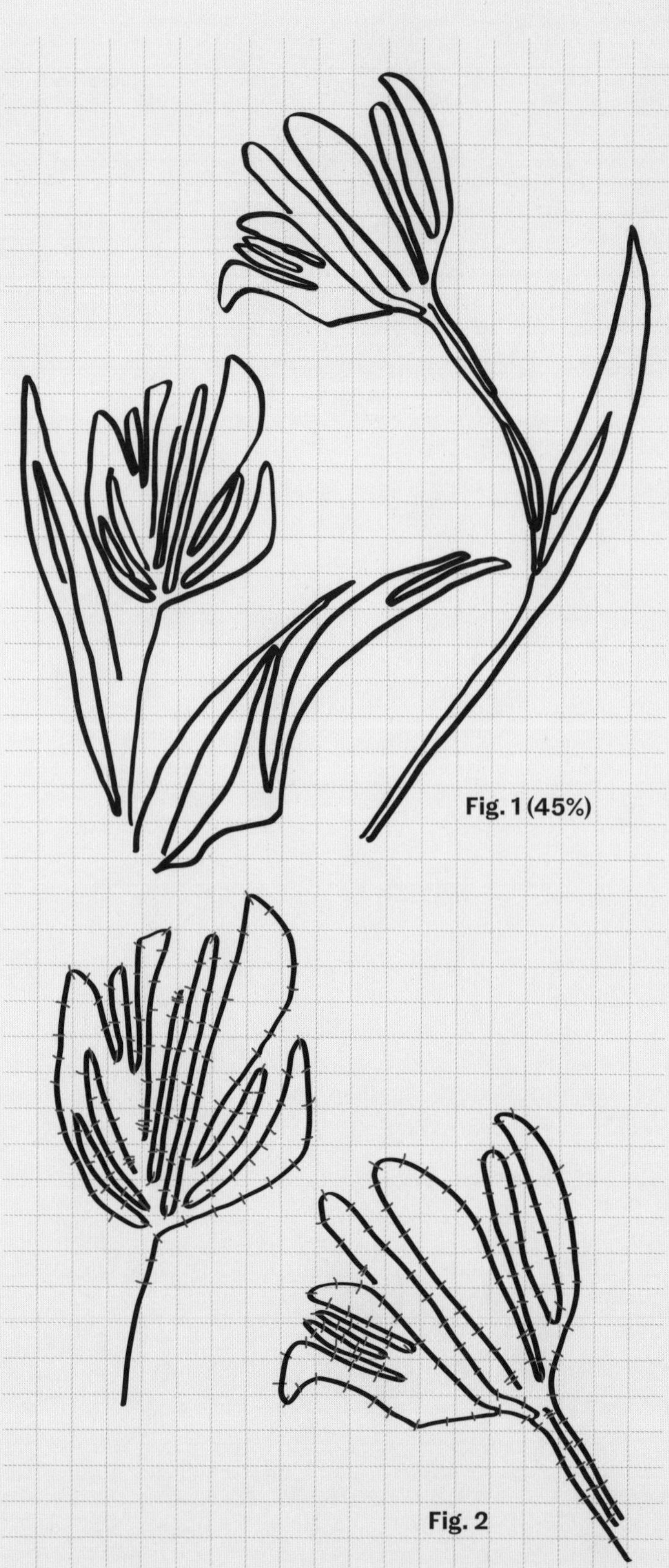

Fig. 1 (45%)

Fig. 2

Flower Stem Blanket

Creating something on a large scale can be daunting, especially with hand embroidery, but the best way to go about it is to break it down into manageable sections. For this project I decided on a few simple flower stems that look as though they have been thrown down on the blanket. These are slightly oversized flowers, and you can easily scale up your design by using thicker materials – here I have used chunky wool yarn for my couched stems and thick strips of silk fabric to make the flowers. You could create this design with any scraps of fabric you have to hand as it is a really good way to recycle material you can't bear to throw away. I have embroidered onto a vintage blanket I found at a carboot (trunk) sale, but you often see old wool blankets in charity shops or thrift stores.

You will need

Template (see page 144)
Scrap paper (to use for template)
Small sharp scissors
Boiled wool blanket
Dressmaking pins
Dissolvable fabric pen (best on this light-coloured fabric, but see page 43 for other options)
Tacking (basting) thread (optional)
Large embroidery needle (or sharp darner needle)
Medium embroidery hoop (see tip on page 66)
Base yarn for the stems: chunky wool yarns in two shades of green
Top threads: embroidery thread (floss) in colours to match the chunky yarn and fabric (use three strands) and standard sewing thread to match your flower fabric
Base yarn for the flowers: strips of fabric or ribbon (if using fabric, cut the strips roughly 3 cm (1 ¼ in) wide, or vary them according to the finish)

TIP
Design your flower heads to fit in the embroidery hoop. I used a 20 cm (8 in) hoop.

1. Copy the flower template **(see page 144)** or draw silhouettes of your flowers and leaf shapes on paper and cut them out.
2. Lay your blanket out flat so you can position and pin the paper templates in place, starting with the flower heads and thinking about where the stems will go (I find it easier to draw a stem in freehand). Using templates means you can move the flowers around and enables you to be more flexible with the design.
3. Hang the blanket up so you can step back from it and make sure you are happy with the placement.
4. Draw around the templates with a fabric pen and add in the stems by hand (or use a template if you prefer). If you find the fabric pen does not work on the blanket, use a large tacking (basting) stitch to mark it out **(see page 44)**.

STEMS AND LEAVES

1. Put your hoop around the end of your stem where you would like to start. You may need to loosen the hoop quite a lot to get the thick material in. If your fabric is too thick, you do not need to use a hoop and can work on it flat on a large table surface.
2. Start the embroidery by working the stems. I used two lengths of light green chunky wool yarn as the base yarn, stitched down next to each other using three strands of embroidery thread (floss) as the top thread, using the basic couching technique **(see page 32)** and lining up the stitches next to each other, roughly 1 cm (½ in) apart.
3. When you have completed the stems, stitch the central veins of the leaves in the same way, using a single length of the same chunky base yarn as your stem **(Fig. 1)**.

Fig. 1

4. Now go around the outer line of the leaf shape (I have just done a simple outline of my leaves) **(Fig. 1)**. You could fill the leaves to make a solid colour by following your line along your leaf shape until you have filled the space.

FLOWER HEADS

1. To make the flowers I used strips of silk in two different patterns as the base yarn. Use the same basic couching stitch, but to make sure the fabric doesn't come loose, stitch into the ends of the fabric strip and at random points along the way to secure it. It is fine to have lots of different types of material in different colours and lengths – this is a great way to use up fabric scraps.

2. For both flower types, I have used a double length of standard sewing thread. Start in the centre of the flower by stitching down the end of the fabric strip or ribbon.

3. For the first flower **(Fig. 1)**, work your way around in a spiral from the centre outwards using basic couching stitch **(see page 32)**. Try not to make the circle too uniform in order to create a more natural flower look. Pull the fabric strip out a bit as you go along, puffing it out between stitches to give a three-dimensional rose shape. I lined up my stitches as I worked my way out, which makes the puffed-up fabric look like layers of petals.

4. For the second flower **(Fig. 2)**, work in a zigzag for the circle at the centre of the flower first, then do the outer circle. Make stitches at the top and bottom of the Z-shaped line, doing a few occasional stitches into the fabric or ribbon to secure it as you go along. When you have finished, stitch into the strip of fabric a few times to secure it in place, and tie it off with a knot.

5. Release the embroidery hoop and reposition it over the next flower, completing all the embroidery in the same way.

Fig. 1

Fig. 2

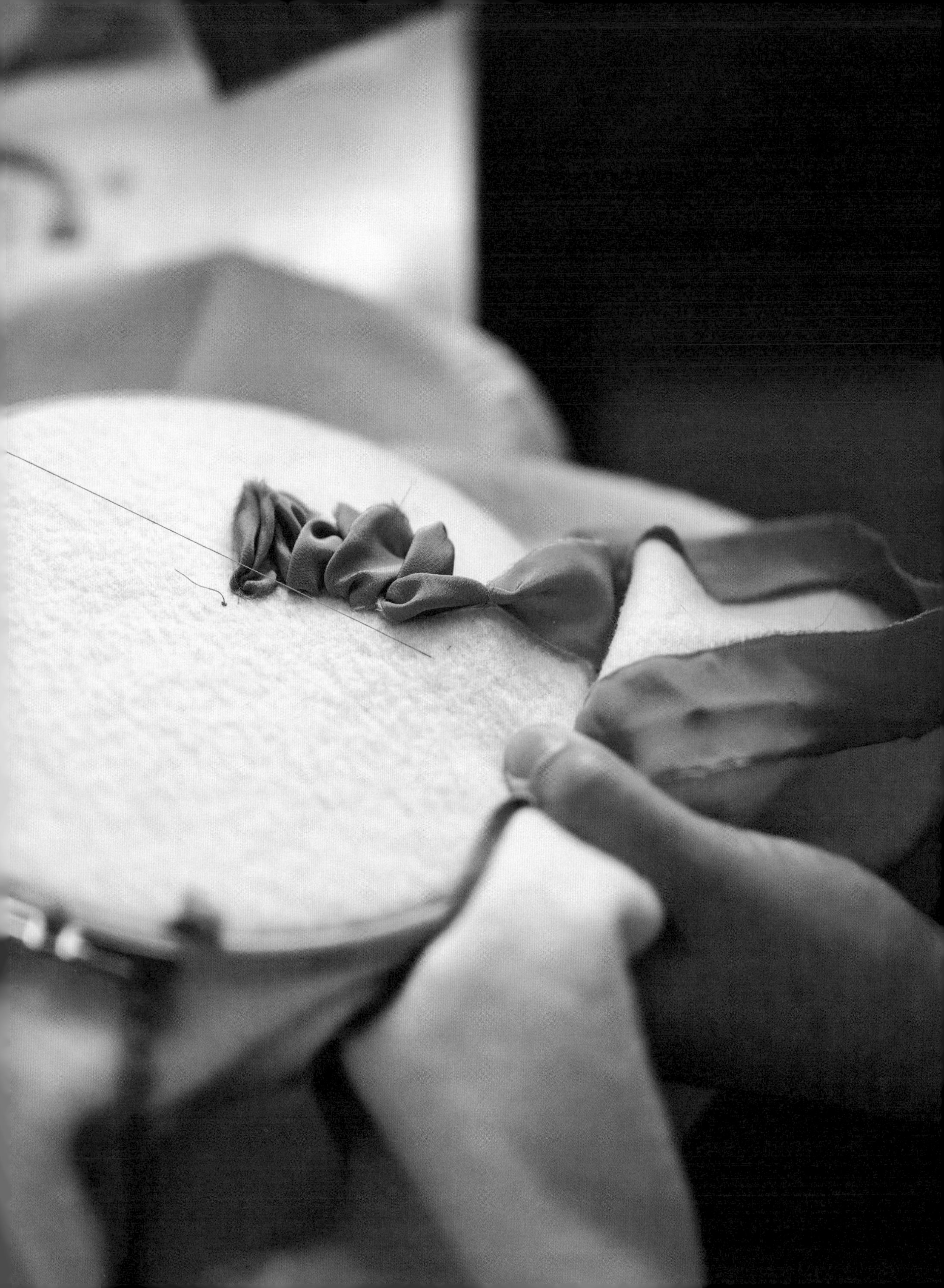

Dandelion Brooch

This brooch is made using a variation on the traditional couching technique — it is not strictly couching, but uses the general principle of anchoring the material to the surface of the fabric. Instead of following a drawing, you are creating the pattern with loops. The same technique could be used directly onto larger fabric pieces. You could work this design using a variety of materials, but I find Russia braid works best for this dandelion.

You will need

Pencil, tailor's chalk or dissolvable fabric pen

Piece of wool felt (or a thick material that will not fray when cut), approximately 3 × 8 cm (1/4 × 3 1/4 in)

Small sharp scissors

Base yarn: Russia braid, 3 mm (1/8 in) wide, in golden yellow

PVA glue

Embroidery or hand sewing needle

Top thread: standard machine sewing thread, to match the Russia braid

Brooch pin

TIP

The smaller inner hoops will become the centre of your flower and the more petals you have on your flower, the more upright and bunched together they will be. I have used a square of thick wool felt to stitch the braid onto, which means there's no need to back the brooch. If you do not have this, I recommend backing your fabric on to card or a thicker material before you turn it into a brooch. Try to match the colour of the fabric to the colour of your braid.

1. Draw out a circle approximately 1.5 cm (⅝ in) in diameter onto the felt fabric – this is your outline for sewing. You can use a pencil or dissolvable pen to draw these freehand.

2. Cut a piece of Russia braid approximately 1.5 m (60 in) long – this will form the flower petal loops. Secure the ends of the braid with glue and allow to dry.

3. Thread a needle with a double length of the top thread.

4. Secure the end of the braid along your drawn line or at any point on your circle by making a couple of small stitches. The end of the braid should be inside your drawn circle.

5. Now loop the braid down and up over the end of the braid in a figure of eight, covering the end. Make a stitch where the braid meets to secure it. Take the braid back down on the right **(Fig. 1)**. The loops inside the circle will form the flower centre, so keep these uniform in size (but smaller than the outer loops).

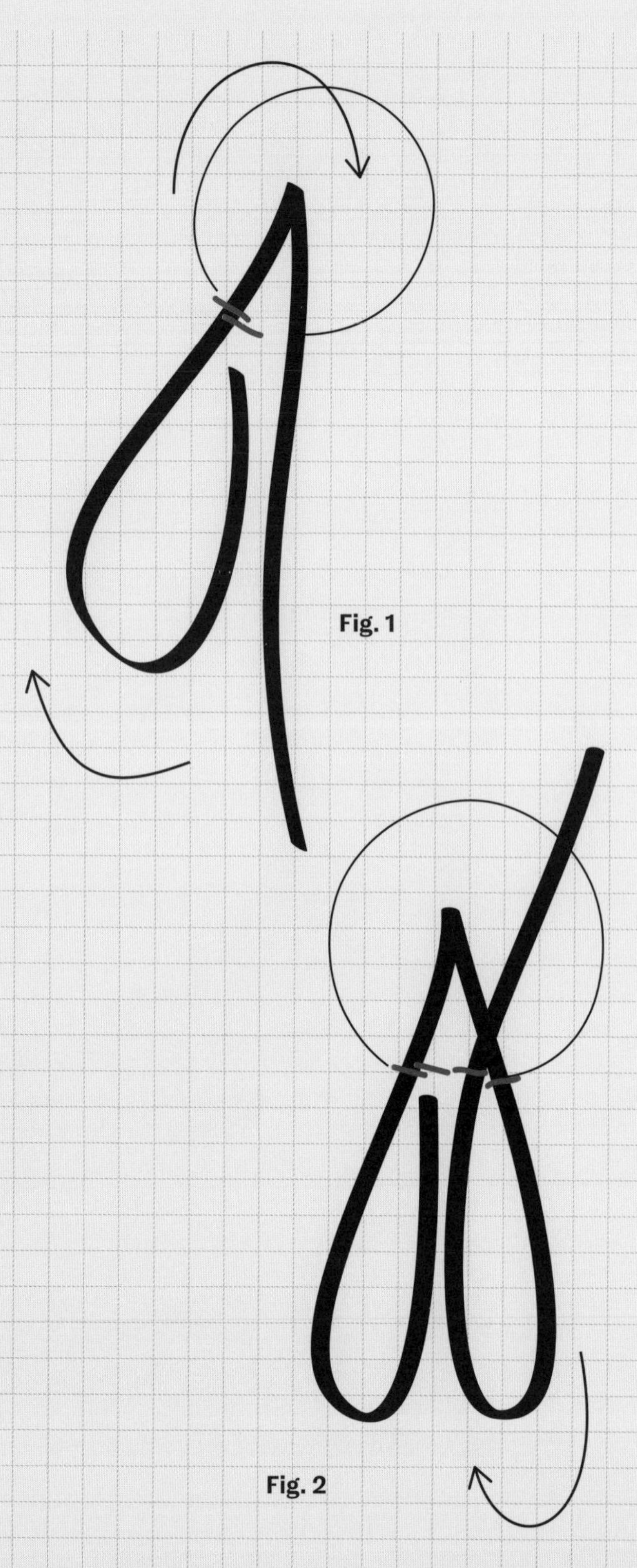

6. Continue the figure of eight with the braid **(Fig. 2)**, stitching down using two back stitches **(see page 33)** over each new loop every time you cross the braid over. Use your non-dominant thumb to hold down the braid and use the other hand to loop it up and down. Your loops should be close together and larger on the lower side of your drawn line than the upper side (the centre of your flower).

7. Repeat the process **(Fig. 3)** until you have gone all the way around the circle to complete your full flower.

8. To finish, make a final small top loop and cut the braid off at double the length of your petal size. Finish the end off with glue. Loop it back towards the flower's centre, hiding it under the petals **(Fig. 4)**. Then stitch into place.

9. When you have completed your flower, go back over all of your stitches one more time in one go, to secure them.

10. To complete the brooch, using small sharp scissors carefully trim the felt at the back of the flower into a circle 3 mm (⅛ in) away from your stitch line. Sew on the brooch pin.

Fig. 3

Fig. 4

Leaf Embroidered Cardigan

A classic wool cardigan is a staple in my wardrobe, and if you have one that needs a bit of love, a great way to do that is with embroidery. My inspirations for this design are cardigans I have found in vintage shops and seen in old photographs from the 1940s and 50s with delicate motifs embroidered onto them. Adding an embroidered detail to a plain cardigan is the perfect way to upcycle a garment; it's even a good way to cover up a moth hole or stain. This motif is inspired by beautiful glass bead leaf shapes I bought in France. By keeping the design simple and repeating it over the cardigan in different autumnal colours, I think it looks both classic and contemporary.

You will need

Template (see page 78)
Small sharp scissors
Dissolvable fabric pen
Wool or cashmere cardigan
Embroidery needle
Tacking (basting) thread (optional)
Base yarn: cotton or silk embroidery thread (floss) or a thin braid
Small embroidery hoop
Top thread: complementary standard machine sewing thread

TIP

I would recommend doing a sample of this design using a variety of materials to see the effects they have on the appearance of the leaves and to work out the scale that suits your garment. If you are stitching onto knitted material, be careful with your tension – do not pull your stitches too tight. Use a hoop very loosely to keep it flat, but do not pull your fabric too tight because your design will go out of shape when it's released from the hoop.

1. Draw your motifs **(Fig. 1)** on your garment with a fabric pen. You can trace these through the fabric **(see page 43)**, but if your fabric is too thick you could tack (baste) a line down the centre of each stalk to give you a guide to work along **(see page 44)**.

2. Once you have your motifs roughly plotted out on your garment, start by selecting your embroidery thread (floss) or thin braid to use as the base yarn.

3. Place the area with the bottom of a stem into the embroidery hoop.

4. If you would like to hide the end of your thread in the fabric rather than leave it loose like I have, follow this step; otherwise skip to step 5. Put your base yarn on to a large needle and tie a knot in the end. Put the needle into the fabric from the back at the bottom of the design, so this will be at the end of the stems of the leaves and remove the needle.

Fig. 1 (100%)

5. Thread up a thinner thread to use as your top thread – I have used a single strand of sewing thread.
6. Use your non-dominant thumb to hold the base thread and stitch it down with your top thread using the basic couching stitch **(see page 32)**.
7. Follow your marked outline up the stem until you reach the leaves, then follow the line in a horizontal figure-of-eight shape, continuing on to the next set of leaves with a small line in between **(Fig. 2)**. Try to do this in one single line of base yarn if possible, without breaks. If you do run out of base yarn, you can hide your ends and start again following the method in step 4.
8. When you reach the top of the first leaf, secure the top thread with a few small stitches at the back of your piece. Finish off the design by hiding the base thread in the fabric as in step 4, putting the embroidery thread (floss) on the needle and through the fabric from the front rather than the back. Finish by tying it off with a knot in the back of the fabric.
9. Repeat these steps until you have finished all three leaves. If you have left ends loose at the bottom of the bunch of leaves, you will be left with a small tassel which is a nice little feature. This can be trimmed down or neatened off using small sharp scissors.

Fig. 2

Framed Chrysanthemum Embroidery

This project is inspired by old botanical illustrations, each one meticulously hand painted with watercolours. I love the faded pastel colours of the plants and delicate lines of the drawings, so for this embroidery I have used very fine threads which give it a drawn quality. Put this in an open-backed frame, and the shadow created when the sun shines through is beautiful. Working on this small scale can seem difficult, and it can certainly be fiddly at points, but if you put your fabric in a small hoop and work along the lines of your design methodically, you will be surprised at how quick and satisfying this can be. I used silk embroidery threads on a very fine and stiff fabric.

You will need

Open-back frame fitted with two pieces of glass, roughly 20 × 30 cm (8 × 12 in)
Dissolvable fabric pen
Cotton organdie (or any sheer light fabric), slightly larger than the frame
Small sharp scissors
Template (see page 85)
Dressmaking pins
Small or medium embroidery hoop
Base yarn: embroidery thread (floss) in four colours (I used silk thread in green and three different tones of yellow)
Large embroidery needle (with a large eye)
Small embroidery needle
Top thread: standard machine sewing thread to match the embroidery threads

TIP

Cut your fabric larger than you need so you can fit it comfortably in the embroidery hoop, then cut it down to suit the dimensions of the frame after you have finished. Think about the thickness of your base yarn in relation to the depth of your frame before going ahead with making. This is why I have used very fine base yarn to make sure it will fit in my frame.

1. Start by working out how big the inner area of your frame is, and mark this out on your fabric using the fabric pen.

2. Draw your design **(Fig. 1)** on your fabric using a fabric pen. You can trace the design from your drawing by placing the fabric on top without a lightbox as the fabric is so thin **(see page 43)**.

3. Place your fabric in the embroidery hoop at the bottom of the stem **(see page 46 for advice on working with very delicate fabric)**.

4. Select the embroidery thread (floss) for your base yarn. If you would like to hide the end of your thread in the fabric rather than leave it loose as I have, follow this step, otherwise skip to the next step. Thread the base yarn for the stem onto a large needle and tie a knot in the end. Put the needle into the back of the fabric at the bottom of the flower stem where you will start your embroidery. Once the thread is through the fabric, take it off the needle.

5. Thread the smaller needle with the top thread and pin the base yarn along the drawn line to start with and then using

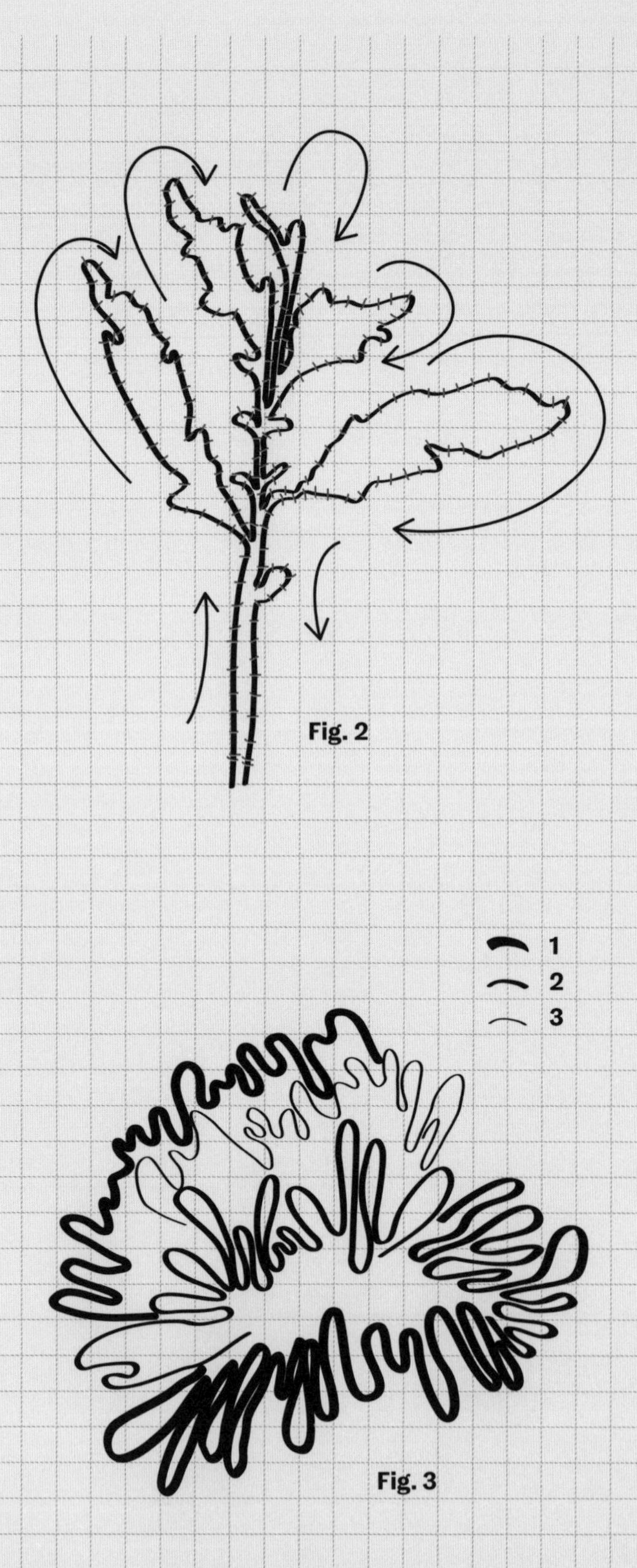

Fig. 2

Fig. 3

your thumb to guide it along the design as you go.

6. Stitch down your base yarn using basic couching stitch **(see page 32)**, working from side to side with the top thread and placing stitches every 3–5 mm (⅛–¼ in). Follow along the lines of the design using one length of top thread if possible. Work up one side of the stem and the leaves from base to flower head, then down the other side **(Fig. 2)** so you end up with the leaf outlines having a single thickness of base yarn and the stem with a double thickness.

7. When you reach the end of the leaf and stem, secure the top thread with a few small stitches in the back of the fabric.

8. Finish off your embroidery by hiding the base thread in the fabric as in step 4. Put the embroidery thread (floss) onto your large needle, pass it through the fabric from the front rather than the back and finish by tying it off with a knot in the back of the fabric.

9. Repeat these steps to create the flower head. For the petal base yarn I used three different tones of embroidery thread (floss) to give the design more depth. In **Fig. 3**, number 1 is the thickest line of three whole lengths of embroidery thread in a lighter yellow, 2 is two lengths of twisted embroidery thread (floss) stitched down together in a darker yellow, and 3 is a single very fine embroidery thread in darker yellow.

10. Once finished, trim the embroidery to size. Wash the water-soluble pen away by placing the embroidery in a clean container with lukewarm water, then leave to dry on a flat surface. Once dry, iron on the back and place into your frame.

Fig. 1 (70%)

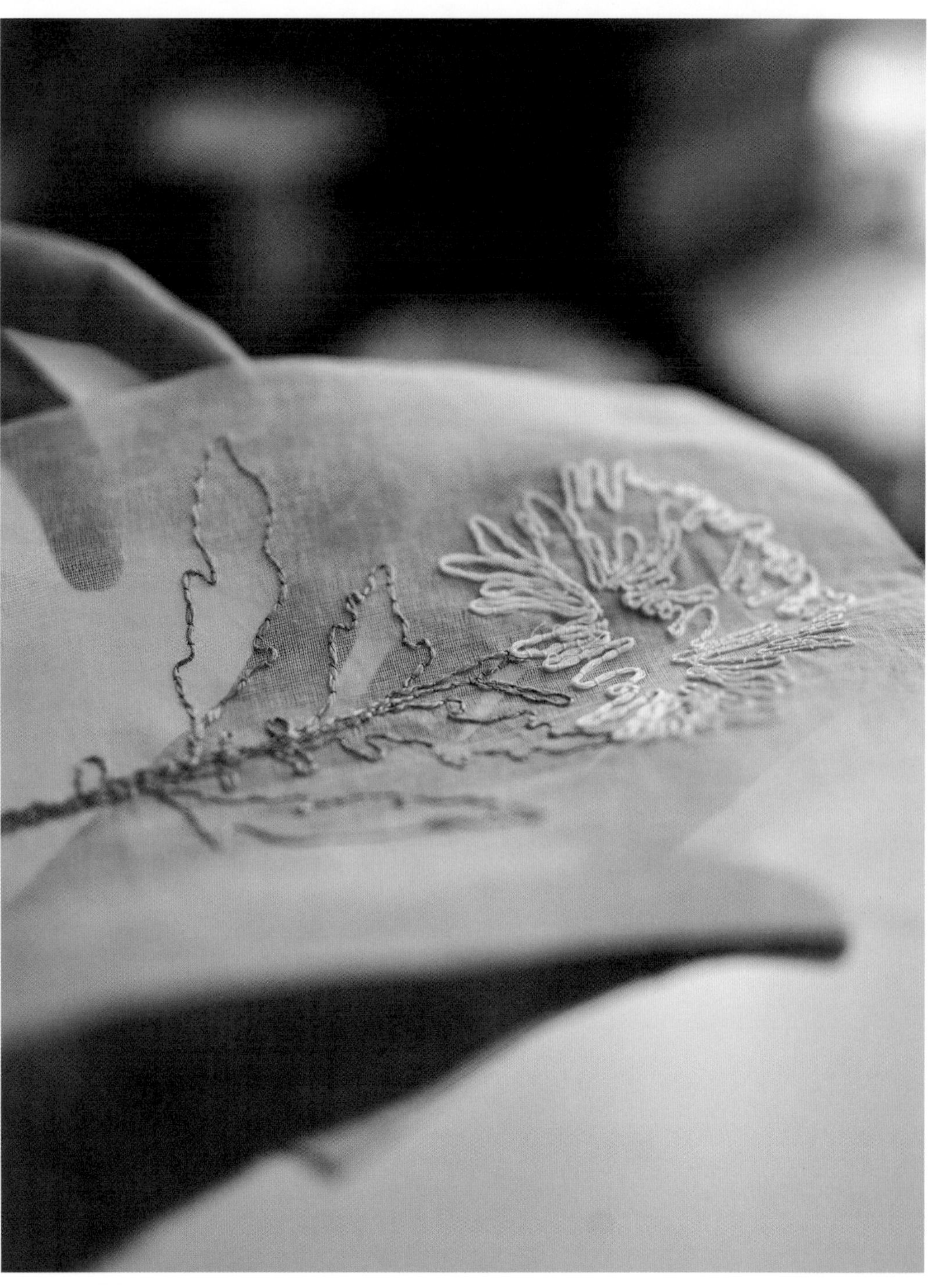

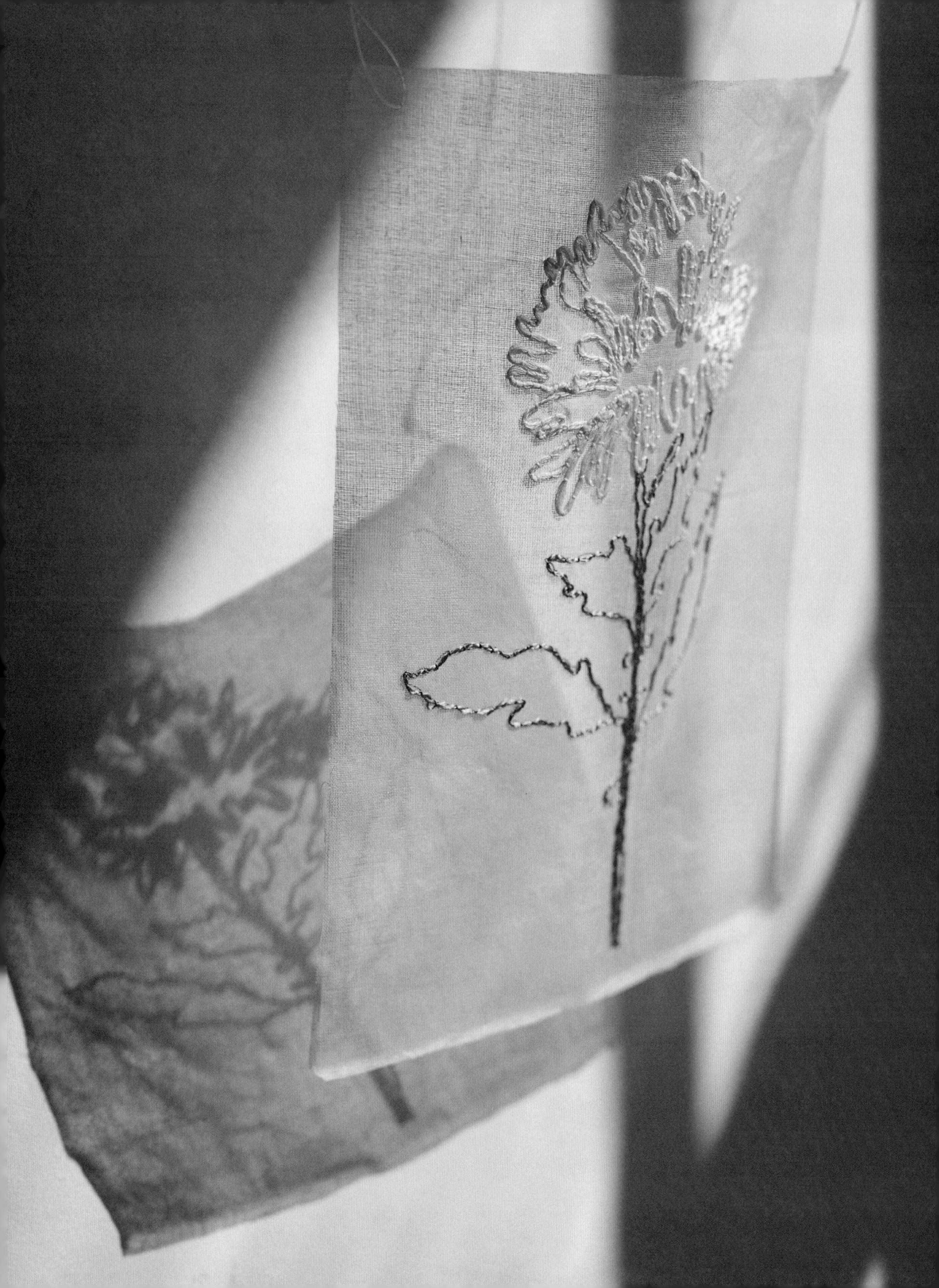

Rudbeckia Linen Curtain

This simple and elegant curtain design is a really beautiful way to add a silhouette of pattern to your window. White on white, this is reminiscent of traditional French lace, and is a great way to add privacy to a window that may be overlooked. The technique could be used on a longer pair of linen curtains, or even a dress for a special occasion. The shadow cast by the embroidered rudbeckia flowers is what I love about this piece, perfect for a sunny window.

You will need

Dissolvable fabric pen
Lightweight linen gauze or cotton lawn fabric in white
Template (see page 145)
Small sharp scissors
Dressmaking pins
Base yarn for stems and leaves: thick cotton yarn such as mercerised cotton embroidery thread (floss) or sashiko thread in white (also used as top thread)
Base yarn for flower petals: bamboo tape (or thin ribbon) in white
Base yarn for flower centres: ric-rac tape in white
Medium to large embroidery hoop
Embroidery needle
Top thread for flower petals and centres: strong cotton sewing thread in white
Large sharp scissors
Sewing machine

1. Draw your design on your curtain using the fabric pen. You can trace the design onto the fabric from the template **(see page 145)**. As the fabric is translucent you can place the drawing underneath or do this freehand **(see page 43)**.

2. Prepare all the base yarns by placing them on your fabric and cutting lengths to fit the parts of your drawing you want to embroider; it can help to pin the stems down before you stitch them in place.

3. Place the embroidery hoop over your starting point. Begin by embroidering the stems and leaves using multiple cotton threads. I used five strands of mercerised cotton embroidery thread (floss) as the base yarn and stitched over the top of it using one strand of the same thread (this thread is thick enough to just use a single strand rather than doubling it up). Thread the needle with the top thread and tie a knot in one end.

4. Start at the bottom of the stem and work your way along the line. Use blanket stitch **(see page 35)** down the stems and outline of the leaves.

5. When the stems and leaves are finished, move on to the flower petals. Thread the needle with a thinner thread, such as a standard strong white cotton thread.

6. Make a couple of stitches in the same place at the beginning of the tape and continue along the lines of your drawing using back stitch **(see page 33)**.

7. Using your drawing as a guide, loop the bamboo tape back and forth in zigzags **(Fig. 1)**. Using bamboo tape as a base yarn means you can open it up to cover larger areas, so try to open it up a little when you reach the tips of the petals and fold it a little tighter at the centre of the flower.

8. Keep going along your drawn petal lines until you get back to the beginning. Finish off the end of the tape with a couple of stitches.

9. To make the flower centres with ric-rac, use the same back-stitch technique as used on the petals. Start by folding the end of the ric-rac under itself and stitch along the centre of the braid. Fill the flower centre with the tape in horizontal lines **(Fig. 2)**, back and forth and folding the tape back when you want to start the next line. Finish the tape off the way you started by folding it under itself and doing a few stitches to secure it.

10. To make the curtain, use your large scissors to cut out your fabric, marking out the length and width on your fabric with a pin or fabric pen and remembering to add seam allowances **(see tip overleaf)**.

11. Heat your iron to the correct heat level for your fabric. If you are sewing this after you have completed your embroidery, ensure you iron the piece on the back, not the front.

12. Press the seams on the vertical sides first. Fold over 1 cm (½ in) and iron

all the way along, and then fold that over again by another 1 cm (½ in) and iron to enclose the raw edge. Pin across the seams every 20 cm (8 in) or so. Sew these folded edges on your machine using a straight stitch.

13. To make the top edge, fold over 1 cm (½ in) and iron, then fold over again by 3 cm (1¼ in). Pin along the seam and machine stitch down the long fold line, close to the edge of the fold and leaving the sides of this top fold open, creating a channel for the curtain wire or dowel to go through.

14. Hem the bottom edge in the same way as the top, but fold over 1 cm (½ in) and iron, then fold over again by 4 cm (1½ in). Pin and machine stitch in place. Hand sew the sides closed on the bottom seam.

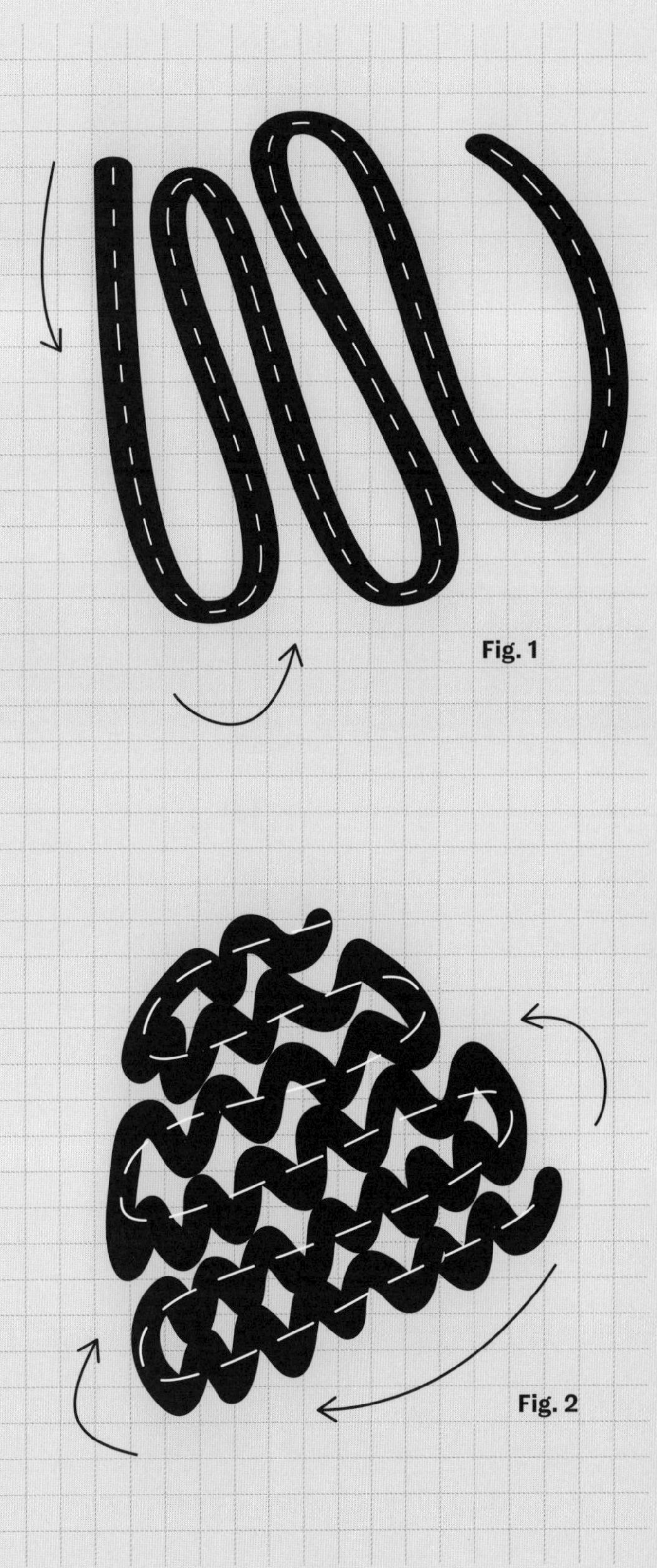

Fig. 1

Fig. 2

TIP

If you're making this curtain from scratch, measure where you want the curtain to sit on your window and add seam allowance to that. I added 2 cm (¾ in) seam allowance on the sides, 8 cm (3¼ in) seam allowance on the bottom and 4 cm (1½ in) on the top.

Tulip Scarf

Tulips are my favourite flower to embroider and they work so well in this single-line drawing due to their long, elegant stems. Tulips have so many different varieties, and their forms change as they wither, when they can be just as beautiful as when freshly cut. For this design I partnered one long stem with leaves and a bud alongside an open flower. For my top thread I used an embroidery thread (floss) that matches the colour of the scarf material so that my stitches will not be seen from the back, but it also means I can make a feature of my stitches on the front.

You will need

Template (see pages 98)
Tracing or scrap paper for template
Small sharp scissors
Dressmaking pins
Tacking (basting) thread (optional)
Embroidery needle
Plain woven wool or cashmere scarf, or a strip of boiled wool cut to roughly 180 × 30 cm (70 × 12 in)
Tailor's chalk (tends to work best on wool)
Medium embroidery hoop
Top thread: embroidery thread (floss) to match the colour of your scarf
Base yarn: chunky wool yarn

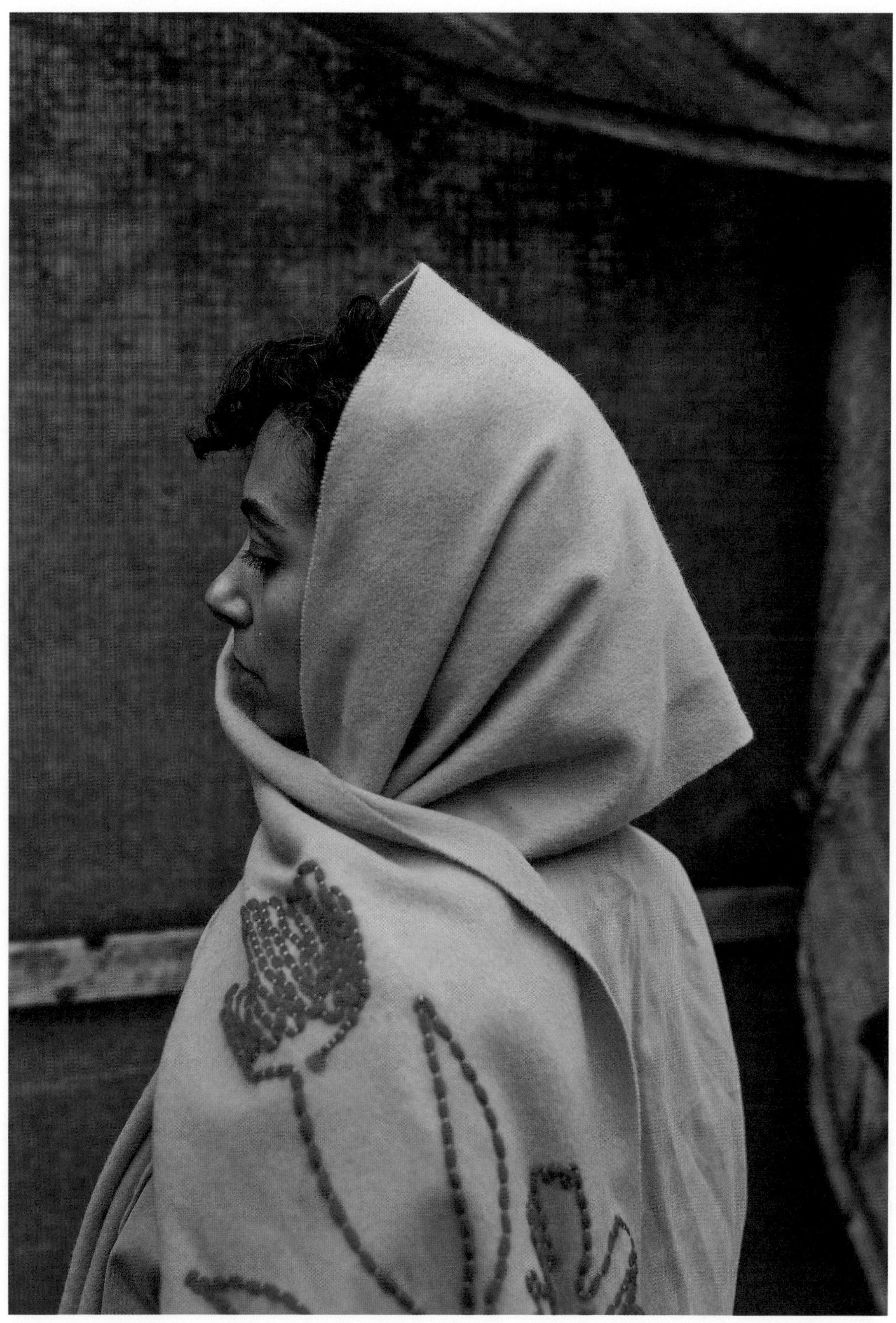

1. Draw or trace your design **(Fig. 1 and 2)** onto paper **(see page 43)**, cut it out and pin it in place on your scarf.
2. Use the tailor's chalk to trace around the shape of the flowers. If you want to be precise about where the lines go, make a stencil **(see page 43)** by cutting out all the lines with a craft knife and go over them with chalk. Alternatively, you can tack (baste) the lines first with large stitches **(see page 44)**. If you are feeling confident, you can mark out the detail inside your flower shapes with chalk freehand.
3. Start by hooping up the open flower **(Fig. 2)** and laying down the base yarn on the drawing.
4. Starting at the centre of the flower, use a couple of pins to secure the base yarn along the first part of the drawn line and work your way out to the petals. I like to start by pinning a small amount, and then use my non-dominant thumb to hold it in place along the rest of the line.
5. Thread your needle with a single length of embroidery thread (floss) (I used three strands of a six-strand embroidery thread), knotting it at one end. Using the basic couching stitch **(see page 32)**, do a couple of stitches over your base yarn at your starting point. Then follow your stencil drawing, spacing the stitches 1 cm (½ in) apart **(Fig. 3)**.
6. When the open flower is complete, finish the embroidery with a final couple of

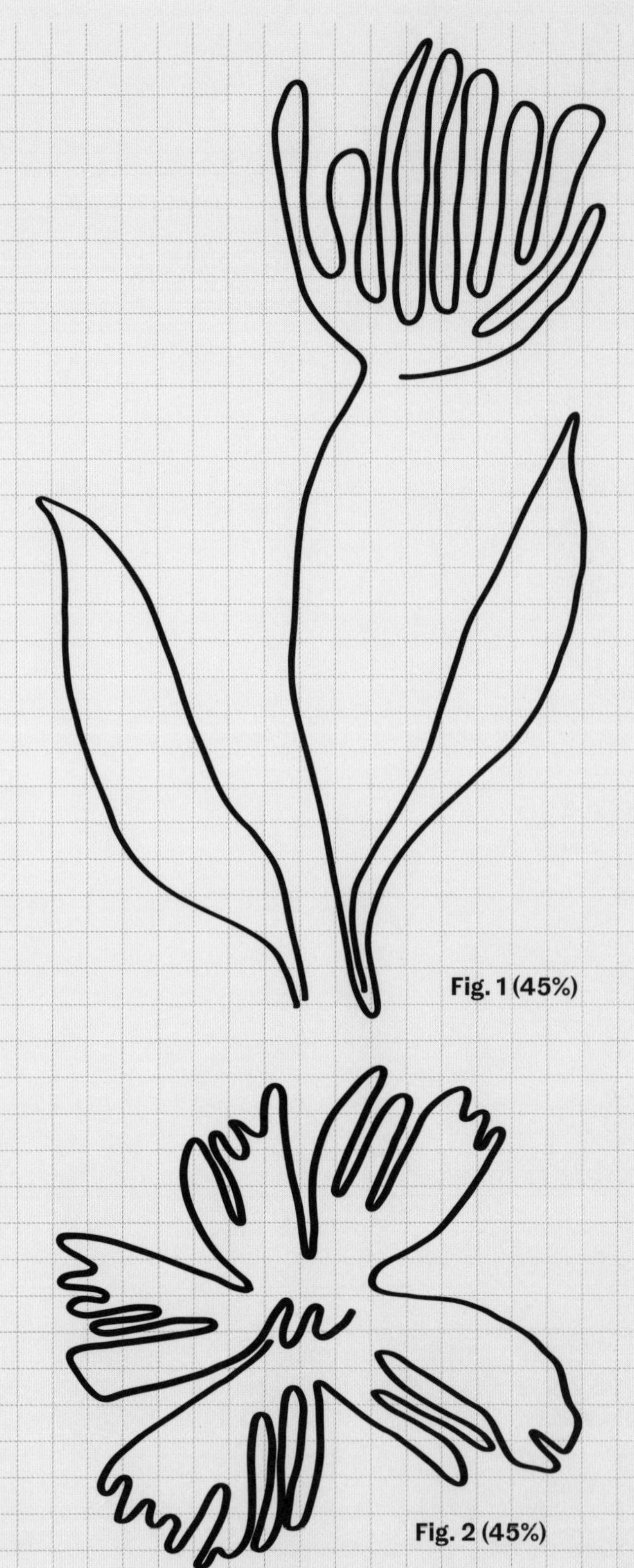

Fig. 1 (45%)

Fig. 2 (45%)

stitches in one place. Put the needle through to the back of the scarf and make a small knot at the back. Trim off the ends of the base yarn.

7. Now move on to stitching the second tulip stem, closed flower and leaves **(Fig. 1)**. Start in the same way as you did with the open flower in step 4 by pinning down the base yarn. Using the basic couching stitch, start at the bottom right-hand side of your leaf and work your way around it first, which will then lead into your stem and up along it to your flower head. Place your stitches 1 cm (½ in) apart.

8. When you reach your flower head, guide the base yarn along the chalk lines in a zigzag, stitching at slightly more regular intervals **(Fig. 4)**, making sure you put a stitch at the point where the line turns back on itself to get a sharp point to your zigzag.

9. Finally, stitch the left leaf in the same way and finish.

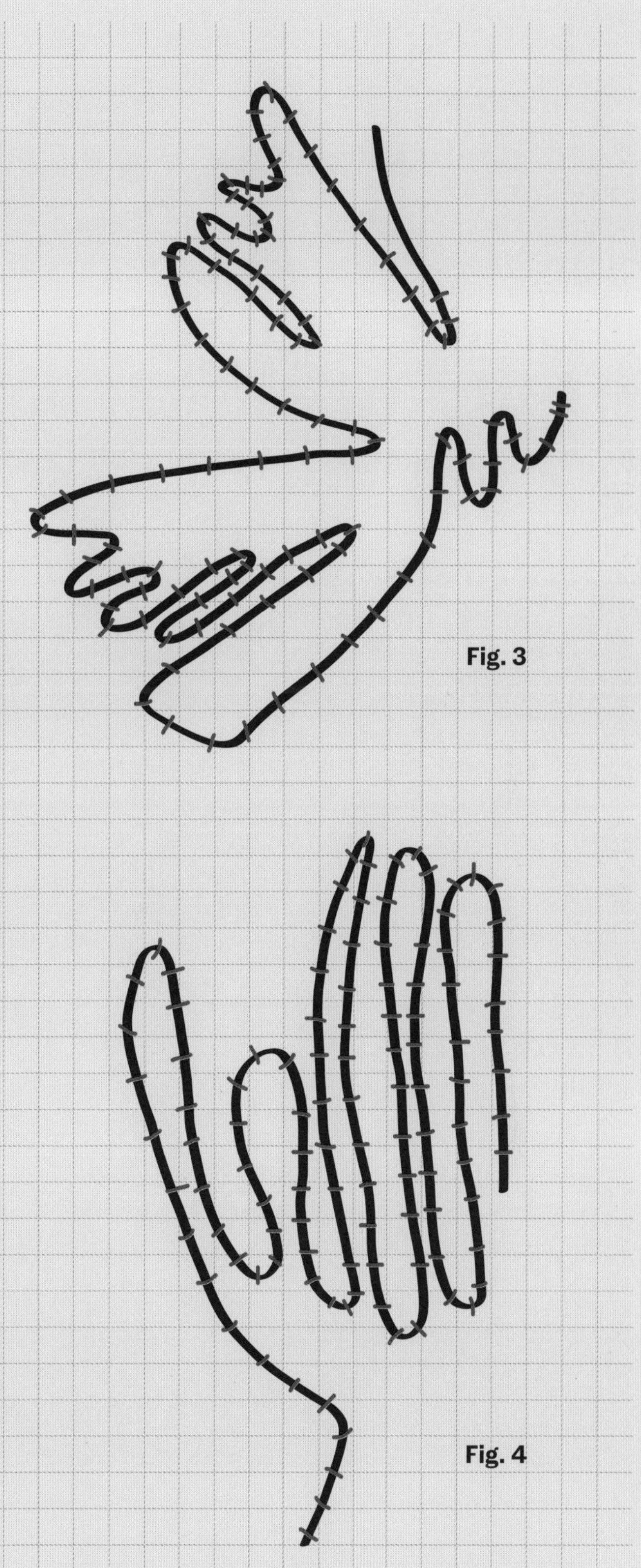

Dahlia Garden Cushion

A lot of my work is inspired by the concept of bringing the garden inside, and this is a celebration of the suburban garden. I have used a mix of Russia braid and stitched-down ribbon, both sewn on using back stitch. By stitching the ribbon down the centre, you are able to widen your line and manipulate it by folding it over into different shapes, using your needle and thread to catch the folds down.

This is a little nod to my love of traditional ribbon work, and I have used vintage ribbon for the large dahlia flower in the centre. To make the leaves for this flower, I have used a green Russia braid and simply outlined the leaf shapes, single lines of braid for stems and have laid the braid in a small row of zigzags for the backs of the flowers.

You will need

Small sharp scissors
Scrap paper, for template
Ruler or measuring tape
Dressmaking pins
Two 40 × 40 cm (16 × 16 in) squares of fabric – I used medium-weight linen
Pencil, chalk or dissolvable fabric pencil
Embroidery needle
Tacking (basting) thread
Template (see page 146)
Base yarn for flowers: ribbon, 1.5 cm (⅝ in) or wider, in cream
Top thread: sewing thread to match the ribbon and braid
Medium embroidery hoop
PVA glue
Base yarn for stems: Russia braid, 4 mm (3⁄16 in) wide, in green and yellow
Hand sewing needle
Sewing machine and thread to match your fabric
Large fabric scissors
Cushion pad (pillow form) – I used natural wool

TIP

Iron the ribbons from the back if you want a flatter design with nice crisp folds or leave it un-ironed for a softer, more three-dimensional finish.

1. To make the template for the cushion, draw a circle on a large piece of paper. If you have a compass or a circular object such as a plate or lampshade that has a diameter of approximately 42 cm (16½ in), you can use that. If not, follow these guidelines.

2. Start by cutting your paper down to a 42 × 42 cm (16½ × 16½ in) square. Fold the paper in half twice so you have a square that is a quarter of the size.

3. Using a ruler, measure 21 cm (8¼ in) from your central point outwards (make sure you measure from the centre of the folds, not the edges of your paper), and mark with your pencil every 2.5 cm (1 in). Join these marks up into a curved line and cut along the line **(Fig. 1)**. Open it out and you have your circle template with a 1 cm (½ in) seam allowance.

4. Pin the template to the front of the fabric, starting from the centre and working outwards, making sure it is flat. Draw around it in fabric pen or chalk, then tack (baste) along this line. Make sure your embroidery is well within 1 cm (½ in) of the circle edge to be inside the seam allowance.

5. Trace your drawing of the large central flower onto the fabric **(see page 43)** using a lightbox or window.

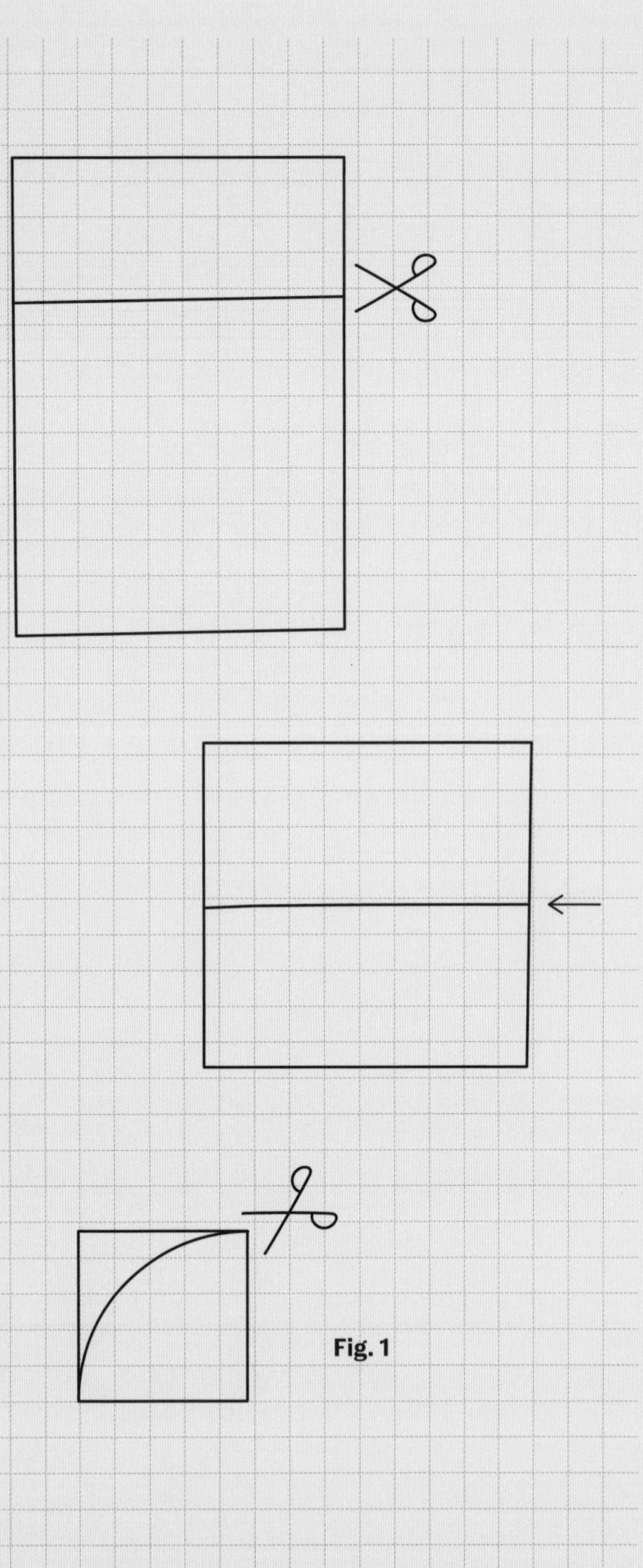

Fig. 1

6. Pin the ribbon over the drawn line of the flower petals **(Fig. 2)**. I find it works best to pin the entire ribbon in place before I start sewing so I can plan where it will turn and fold. Make sure that the ribbon ends are sealed and folded under themselves to hide any frayed edges before you start.
7. Thread the needle with a double length of a standard sewing thread that matches the ribbon and knot the ends together.
8. Place the fabric in the embroidery hoop, fitting the entire design in if you can, otherwise work on it in sections. This may mean you will have to also pin the ribbon down in sections as you work.
9. Using back stitch **(see page 33)**, start by stitching over the folded end of the ribbon a few times to secure it in place, and work your way along the pinned ribbon petals. When working with wide ribbon, I often do two lines of stitching down a petal if I think it needs to be more securely attached **(Fig. 3)**.
10. Work your way along the ribbon back and forth in zigzags, opening up the ribbon to cover wider areas of space or folding it to make it smaller. Try to open up the ribbon more at the centre of the petals and make it smaller at the tips and centre of the flower **(Fig. 3)**. This variation in the line makes it more three-dimensional.
11. Use this same technique to stitch the two smaller buds, with two or three shorter petals placed closer together.

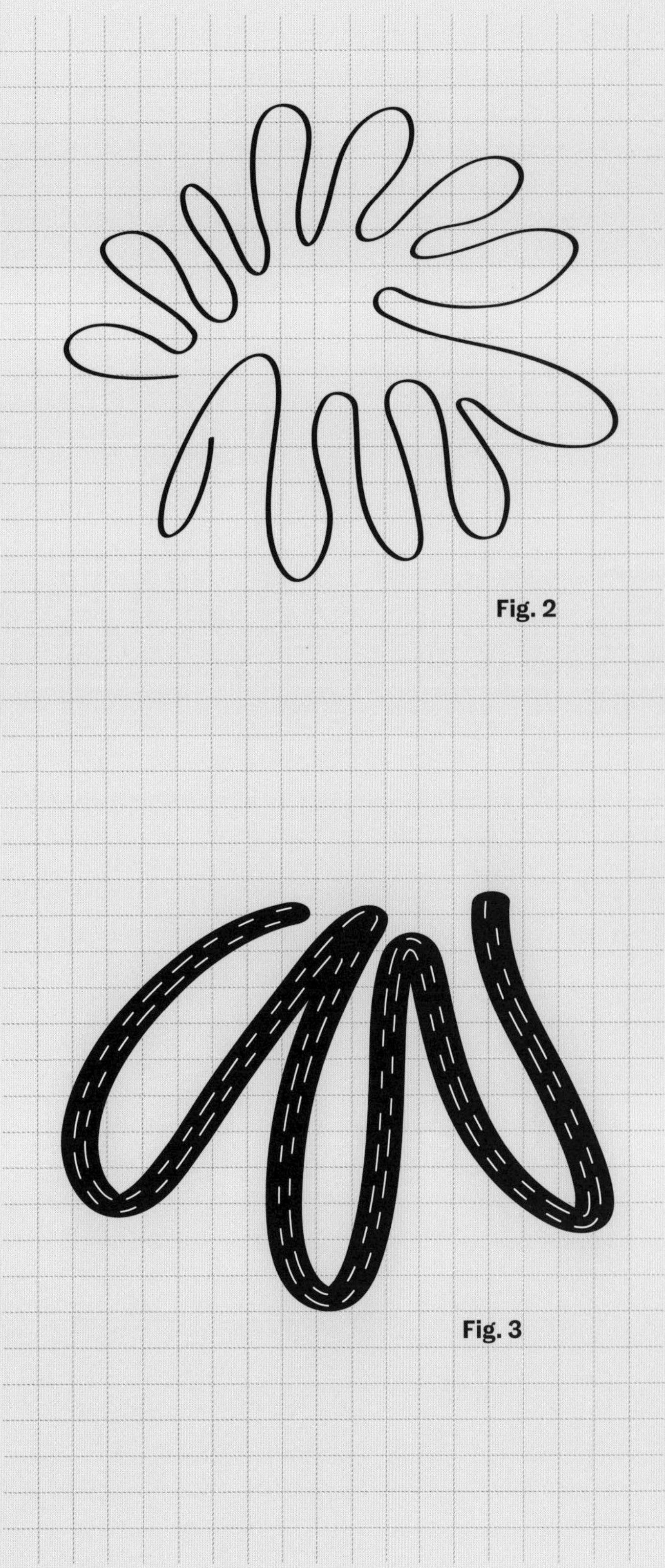

Fig. 2

Fig. 3

12. To create the large flower centre, use yellow Russia braid in a zigzag pattern, working your way back and forth in short lengths around the centre to fill it. Use the template **(see page 145)** as a pattern guide and use back stitch **(see page 33)**.

13. To stitch the leaves, place the embroidery hoop around your drawn leaf. Fix the end of the braid using glue and fold it back on itself before it dries to conceal the end. Lay the braid along the drawn line and pin in place.

14. Thread your needle with a double length of a standard sewing thread that matches the braid and knot the ends together. Using back stitch, start by doing a couple of stitches in place at the folded end of the braid and work your way along the centre until you get to the end of your design.

15. Stitch the stems in the same way as you created the leaves. Glue and fold the visible end under itself as you did at the start and do a few stitches there to finish. Iron your work on the back on an appropriate heat for your fabric and use the steam setting if you want to flatten your embroidery.

16. To make up the cushion (pillow) cover, place your finished embroidered fabric on top of the back fabric with the right sides facing each other (so the back of your embroidery is facing outwards).

17. Mark out your seam allowance by measuring 1 cm (½ in) into your circle and make chalk or pencil dashes every 2.5 cm (1 in) and then join these up. This will give you a guide of where to sew.

18. Make sure your fabrics are lying flat together and pin them together along this drawn line at regular intervals. When working with a sewing machine, it is best to pin across the line rather than directly along it so the needle can slip past it and there is less risk that it will break.

19. Machine stitch along the line, leaving an open gap in the circle of about 10 cm (4 in) – this is for turning the cover right side out and stuffing it.

20. Before you turn it right side out, iron the stitch line. Using fabric scissors, cut along the outer circle you marked out with tacking (basting) thread.

21. Snip small 'V' shapes out of the seam allowance at 3 cm (1¼ in) intervals, making sure you stay 2–3 mm (⅛ in) away from your stitches. This will make the circle shape of the cushion smoother. Turn the cover right side out by pulling it through the unsewn gap.

22. Stuff the cover with your filling. I used waste wool, but you could use synthetic filler, or remnants of wool, fabric scraps or threads as a way of re-using waste. Stitch up the gap by hand with a whip stitch **(see page 38)**.

Fern Leaf Embroidery

This is such a nice way to capture a leaf shape, and ferns are my favourite leaf by far. The design of this piece is inspired by pressed leaves and is a really simple and repetitive but satisfying piece to make. The loose waves of the leaves are created using lengths of multiple silk threads, which have an incredible glow against the matt linen background. This couching technique is not practical for clothing or cushions because it is so loose, but works perfectly in a wall hanging where the threads won't get caught and pulled.

You will need

Template (see page 151)
Small sharp scissors
Dressmaking pins
Linen or any fabric you want to work on
Dissolvable fabric pen and/or tailor's chalk
Top thread: sewing thread to match the silk strands
Embroidery needle
Small or medium embroidery hoop
Base yarn: silk strands (I used waste yarn, but you can use multiple lengths of any soft fine yarn or embroidery thread (floss)

1. Draw the lines of the leaf onto the fabric using an air-soluble pen **(see page 43)**. This is quite a delicate embroidery so better not to wash any marks off.

2. Thread the embroidery needle. I have used a full strand of embroidery thread (floss) for the top thread in a shade to match the base yarn. Tie a knot at one end of the embroidery thread (floss).

3. Place the fabric in the embroidery hoop.

4. The design is broken up into leaf sections. You can join these together at points along the stem.

5. Place the base yarn on the drawn line, starting at the bottom of the stem. Put the needle in from the back of the fabric on one side of the base yarn, holding it down with your non-dominant thumb.

6. Stitch along the stem using basic couching stitch **(see page 32)**, spacing stitches roughly 1.5 cm (5/8 in) apart until you reach the top of the first section of your stem.

7. Now take your stitches to the right, using a small running stitch **(see page 36)** with very wide gaps between the stitches. With each stitch you are catching down the base yarn and then looping it up or down in a wide wave shape as you go **(Fig. 1)**. Taper the waves so they are wide when close to the stems and get gradually smaller as they reach the tip of the leaf.

8. When you have reached the end of the first leaf section, do a few stitches in one place and cut off the end of the base yarn. Start again at the next section of the stem (repositioning the embroidery hoop if necessary), butting the base yarn of the new stem and leaf close to the top of the last part of the stem **(Fig. 2)**.

9. Keep going along each part of the leaf, moving the hoop as necessary and getting gradually smaller as you reach the top of the leaf. Once finished, remove the hoop, lightly iron the back of the fabric and cut away any loose threads.

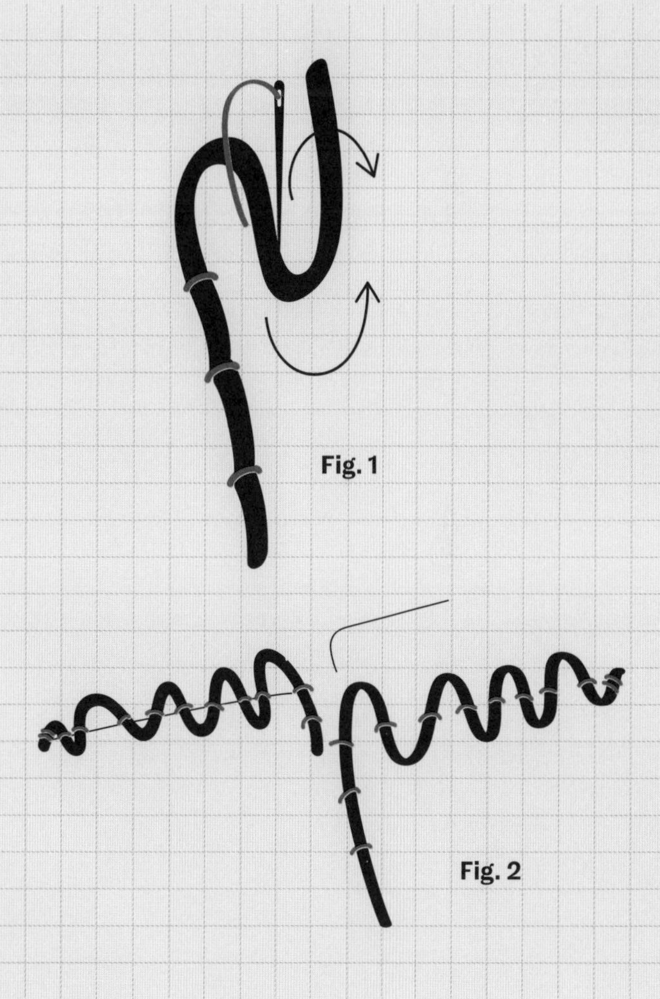

Little Flowers Napkin Set

There is something very nice about having a cloth napkin – it's such a simple way to make a meal feel more special. These embroidered flowers are very quick to complete, and you could try varying the designs with different colours, or by adding more petals to the flowers. You could also take design elements from other projects, such as the table runner on page 124 to make them match.

You will need

Template (see page 114)
Pencil, tailor's chalk or dissolvable fabric pen
Small sharp scissors
Dressmaking pins
4 ready-made napkins
Small embroidery hoop
Base yarn: embroidery thread (floss) in your choice of colours
Large embroidery needle (with a large eye to fit the base yarn through)
Standard embroidery needle
Top thread: complementary or matching sewing thread

1. To create the first flower **(Fig. 1)**, start by drawing the flower on one corner of a napkin using a fabric pen. You can trace it using a lightbox or window **(see page 43)** or you could draw it freehand.

2. Put your fabric into your embroidery hoop – the whole flower should fit inside the hoop.

3. Hide the end of the base yarn in the fabric at the end of an outer edge of a petal. To do this, thread the base yarn onto a needle with a large eye. Put a knot in the end of the thread and feed the needle through the fabric from the back at the end of a drawn line. Leave your needle on the end of the thread and pin it into the fabric somewhere out of the way.

4. Thread a needle with a length of top thread – I have used two strands of a six-strand embroidery thread (floss). Tie a knot at one end of the thread.

5. Stitch down the base yarn on the first petal with a basic couching stitch **(see page 32)**, with small stitches 5 mm (¼ in) apart.

6. When you get to the end of that petal, take the thicker needle, still threaded with base yarn, and push it through from front to back at the end of the drawn line, then bring it up to the front of the fabric at the start of your next petal line **(Fig. 2)**. Continue along your petal edges like this until you have completed them all. You could add more rows to this or finish it here.

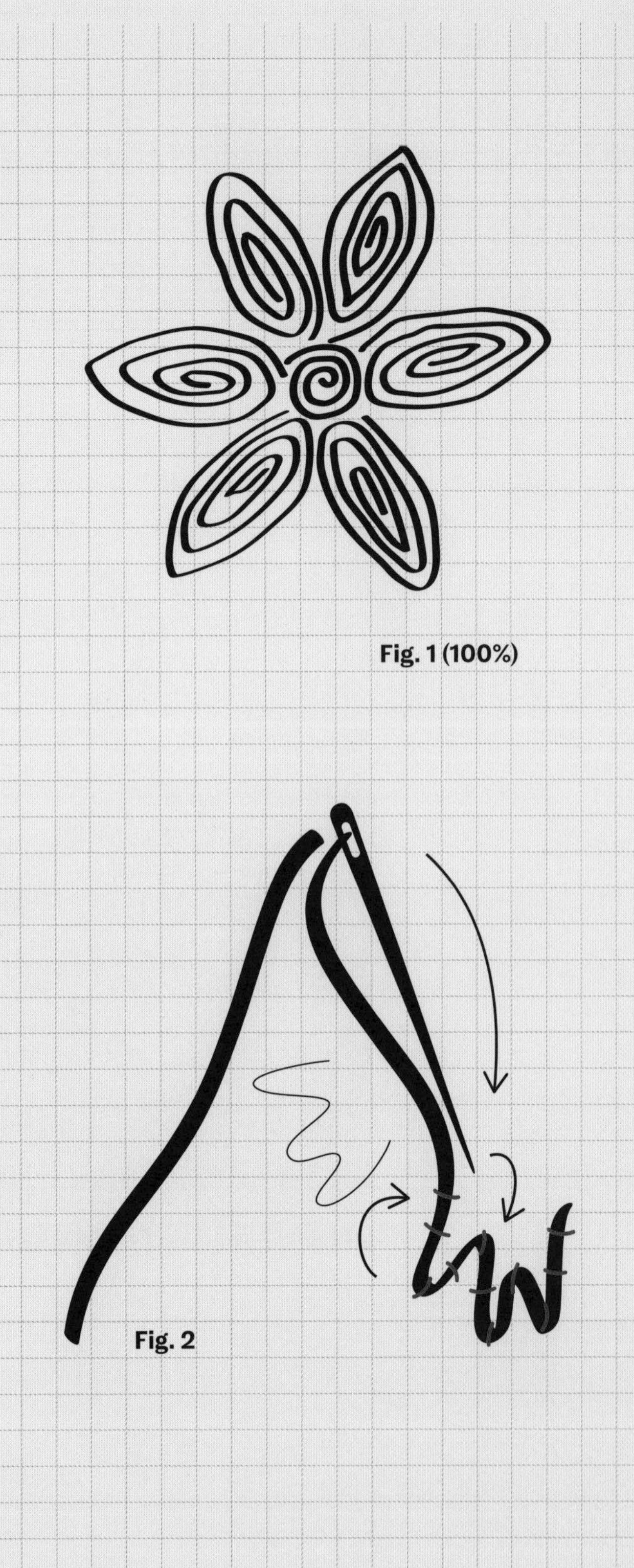

Fig. 1 (100%)

Fig. 2

7. To create the inner edges of the petals, change the base yarn on the bigger needle to the relevant colour and hide the end in your fabric as in step 3. Thread a needle with a new top thread to match. Stitch the inner line in the same way in one long thread without breaks. Hide the end of the base yarn as before.

8. To finish this flower centre, stitch three small French knots **(see page 37)** in a yellow embroidery thread (floss).

9. For the filled petals of the second flower **(Fig. 3)**, start from the bottom left side of your petal, hiding the base yarn in the fabric as in step 3. Thread a needle with the top yarn in the same or different colour thread and use basic couching stitch to work your way along the outline of your petal. Continue filling the petal in a clockwise direction **(Fig. 4)**. Lay the base yarn parallel to your first outline as you work your way around. Finish in the centre of the petal by hiding the end of the base yarn in the fabric and tying it off there.

10. To stitch the centre of the filled-in petal, change your base yarn and top thread again and start in the centre of the flower, working your way around the circle and out in a coil using basic couching stitch, finally hiding the end of the base yarn in the fabric when you have filled the centre and tying it off at the back.

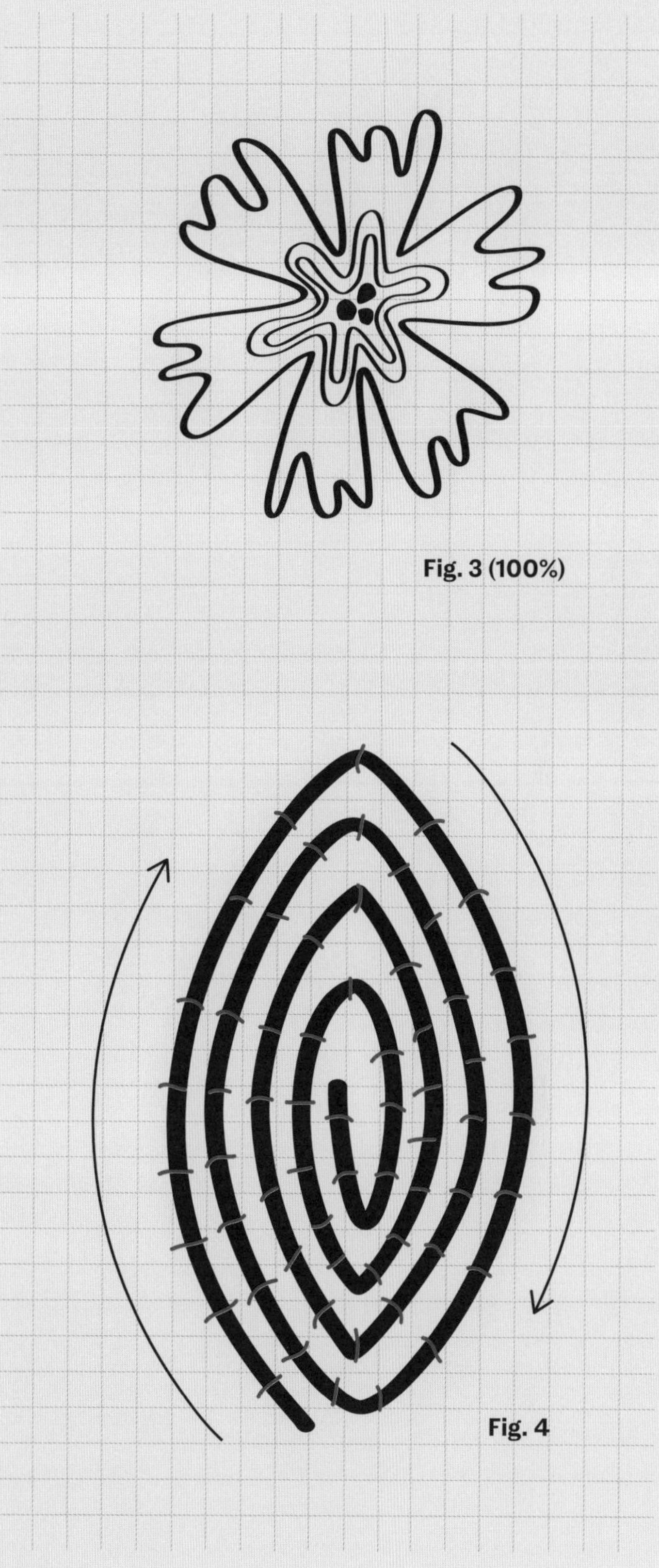

Fig. 3 (100%)

Fig. 4

Carnation Waistcoat

This child's waistcoat is inspired by my ongoing fascination with folk costume, in particular delicately embroidered Ottoman and Eastern European waistcoats as these regions often feature cording and floral patterns in their designs. This home-made version would be a great addition to a child's dressing up box. I have used one technique in three different ways on this piece, using the stitches to create the centre of the flower and the lengths of wool yarn as the petals.

You will need

Template (see page 147)
Dissolvable fabric pen or tailor's chalk
Small sharp scissors
Waistcoat – I made mine from Simplicity pattern 1568, using wool felt with additional cotton binding and ric-rac
Medium embroidery hoop
Wool felt scraps, for leaves
Top thread: embroidery thread (floss)
Large embroidery needle (no. 3)
Base yarn for heart: cotton embroidery thread (floss)
Base yarn for larger flower: fine wool tapestry yarn
Base yarn for small flowers: wool yarn – I used twisted knitting yarn
Base yarn for half flowers: wool yarn – I used twisted knitting yarn

First draw your pattern – you can create a template **(see page 147)**. Use a fabric pen or chalk to draw this out on your fabric **(see page 43)**.

Hoop up the part you want to stitch and follow the steps below for each element of the design.

LEAVES

1. On the back of the waistcoat, I have used the appliqué technique to attach the small, hand cut, felt leaf shapes with a small whip stitch **(see page 38)** around the edges using a matching standard sewing thread. You could also use a blanket or running stitch **(see pages 35 and 36)** around the edges to finish these leaves, or just a single running stitch through each centre would work.

HEART SHAPE WITH LEAVES

1. For the main heart shape on the front of the waistcoat use the basic couching technique **(see page 32)** with one length of cotton embroidery thread (floss).
2. Once you have stitched your heart shape down, add the leaves made from scraps of wool in the same way as described in the Leaves section above.

STEMS

1. For the stems, I used the basic couching embroidery technique **(see page 32)** over five lengths of wool yarn, doing a single stitch over the yarn every 5 mm (¼ in).
2. Start at the bottom of this stem by stitching over five strands of wool yarn, then two lengths come away to form the lower set of branches, and as the stem progresses up towards the largest flower, two more of the embroidery threads branch off to become the upper stems, leaving a single length in the centre for the largest flower. You could pin this out to start with.

LARGE CENTRAL FLOWER

1. The large flower at the top is made using the exact same technique as the small flowers, but with 6.5 cm (2½ in) lengths of multiple fine wool yarn as the base yarn. There are eight individual tufts making up the petals of the flower, and for each of those you need roughly 16 lengths of wool yarn. You could do more or less depending on the thickness of your material and size of your flower.
2. Follow the instructions for the small flower, but with one small addition – because this is on a larger scale, add one more stitch to the centre of your tufts of yarn to keep it in place.
3. Finally, use your small sharp scissors to trim the edges of your flower.

SMALL FLOWER

1. To make the small wool flowers in the lower part of the design, cut eighteen 3 cm (1¼ in) lengths of wool yarn and

put them together in six groups of three. You could also do this with more strands of wool or chunkier wool to get a fuller pompom-like flower.

2. Place one set of three across your circle, making sure you have the line running through the middle of the yarn.

3. Thread the needle with embroidery thread (floss) and knot one end of it. I used the full six strands of thread. Holding the yarn down with your non-dominant thumb, start by putting your needle into the fabric from the back, just to the right of your wool, directly through your drawn circle line.

4. Pull your thread through the fabric and take it over to the left of the base yarn, then put the needle back down into the fabric 2–3 mm (⅛ in) along the line from where you started **(Fig. 1)**.

5. Come up through the fabric from the back again at a point along your line which is about half the width of your yarn.

6. Fold the other side of the yarn over on itself to form the little loop at the centre of your flower and stitch that down by putting your needle back down between your folded yarn. Use running stitch **(see page 36)** over the first part and then back stitch **(see page 33)** over the second part of the yarn fold.

7. When you come up again through the fabric to stitch down the next bundle of yarn, come up right next to your last stitch **(Fig. 2)** so they all sit tightly next to one another.

8. Continue this along your circle line – you may need more lengths of yarn than I have used depending on how tight your stitches are and the thickness of your yarn. When you get to the end, do a few stitches over your last bit and tie a small knot at the back of your fabric. Repeat to make a matching flower on the other side of the waistcoat.

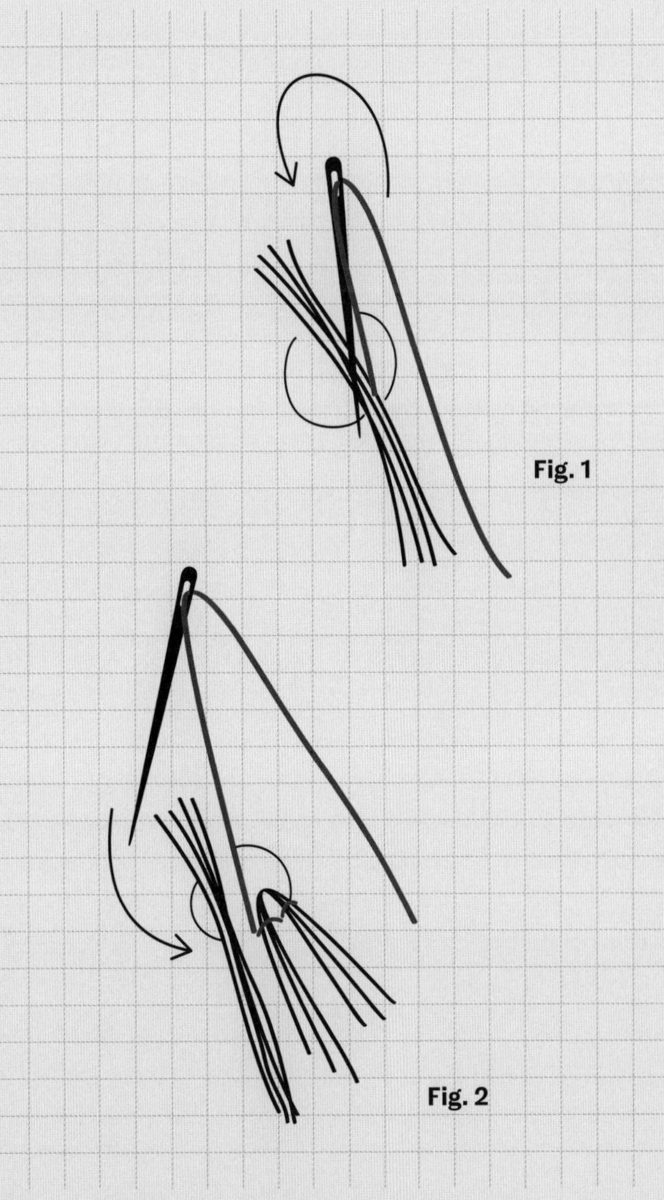

HALF CARNATION

This half flower is the last variation on the same theme. This time we are working in a 'V' shape with lots of lengths of wool. I have cut eighteen 6.5 cm (2½ in) lengths of yarn for each row. There are six rows in total, with three strands in each.

1. Start by laying your multiple lengths of yarn along one side of the 'V', making sure the centre of the yarn is at the point so it is even on both sides.

2. Thread the needle with embroidery thread (floss) and knot one end of it. I have used the full six strands of thread.

3. Holding the base yarn down with your non-dominant thumb, put the needle into the fabric from the back at the top of the left side of the 'V'. Pull the thread through the fabric and take the needle over to the right of the yarn.

4. Put the needle back in the fabric very close to where you started and continue to the next stitch, taking the stitches from left to right over the yarn to secure it.

5. Once you have gone up the other side of the 'V' shape, mirroring your stitches on either side **(Fig. 1)**, add the next row of yarn and start again as you did at the beginning but from the opposite side **(Fig. 2)**. Work like this back and forth for each row, until you have filled the shape. Line up your stitches.

6. Complete the final stitch by stitching over in the same place a few times and tying a knot at the back of the fabric. You can neaten up the fringe flower by trimming the ends with small sharp scissors and use a comb to smooth out the wool. Repeat to make a matching flower on the other side of the waistcoat.

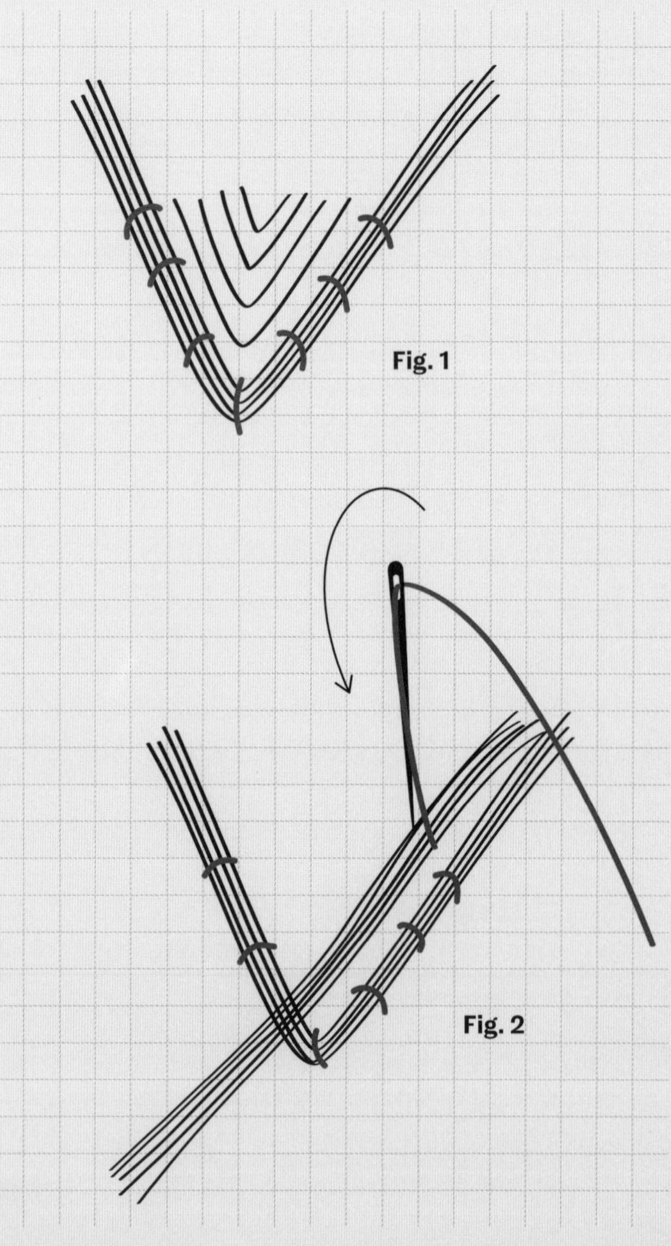

Fallen Leaves Table Runner

A table runner is a simple and elegant way to dress your table, especially if you are sitting outside on a summer evening. The leaf designs are inspired by a combination of real leaves and leaf designs I found on vintage clothing, with little twirly details running down the centres. The leaves are dotted at random over the cloth – spreading your design like this ensures all your guests get to see your beautiful handiwork. I have embroidered onto a readymade table runner in a beautiful moss green, using braids in contrasting and matching tones. I really like working in monotones; they can look very understated.

You will need

Template (see pages 128, 147 and 151)
Pencil, chalk or dissolvable fabric pen
Small sharp scissors
Readymade fabric table runner
Dressmaking pins
Medium embroidery hoop
Embroidery needle
Top thread: complementary or matching sewing thread
Base yarn: Russia braid in various greens or autumnal colours (soft braid, wool yarn or ribbon also work well – see page 26 for material ideas)
PVA glue

TIP

If you have braid on a roll, do not cut it when you start the project – just unroll 50 cm (20 in) to save wasting any.

1. Plan where you want the leaves **(Fig. 1–3 and pages 147 and 151)** to appear on your table runner, then draw them on to the fabric **(see page 43)**.
2. Starting at one end of your cloth, attach the embroidery hoop around the first leaf design.
3. Thread your needle with double-length sewing thread and knot ends together.
4. Glue the end of the braid to prevent it from fraying.
5. Place the braid at one corner of the leaf and make a couple of stitches at the end of the braid. If the drawing is a continuous line, you can cover the glued end over when you have completed the leaf with the final end of the braid folded back on itself. If your line is independent and does not join another, fold this end under itself and stitch it down first.
6. Stitch the braid down using back stitch couching **(see page 33)**. You can pin the first part to start with and then use your non-dominant thumb to guide the braid as you go along. Continue to stitch down your braid, until you are finished.
7. Repeat for all of your leaves using a variety of tones of braid and moving the embroidery hoop as necessary.

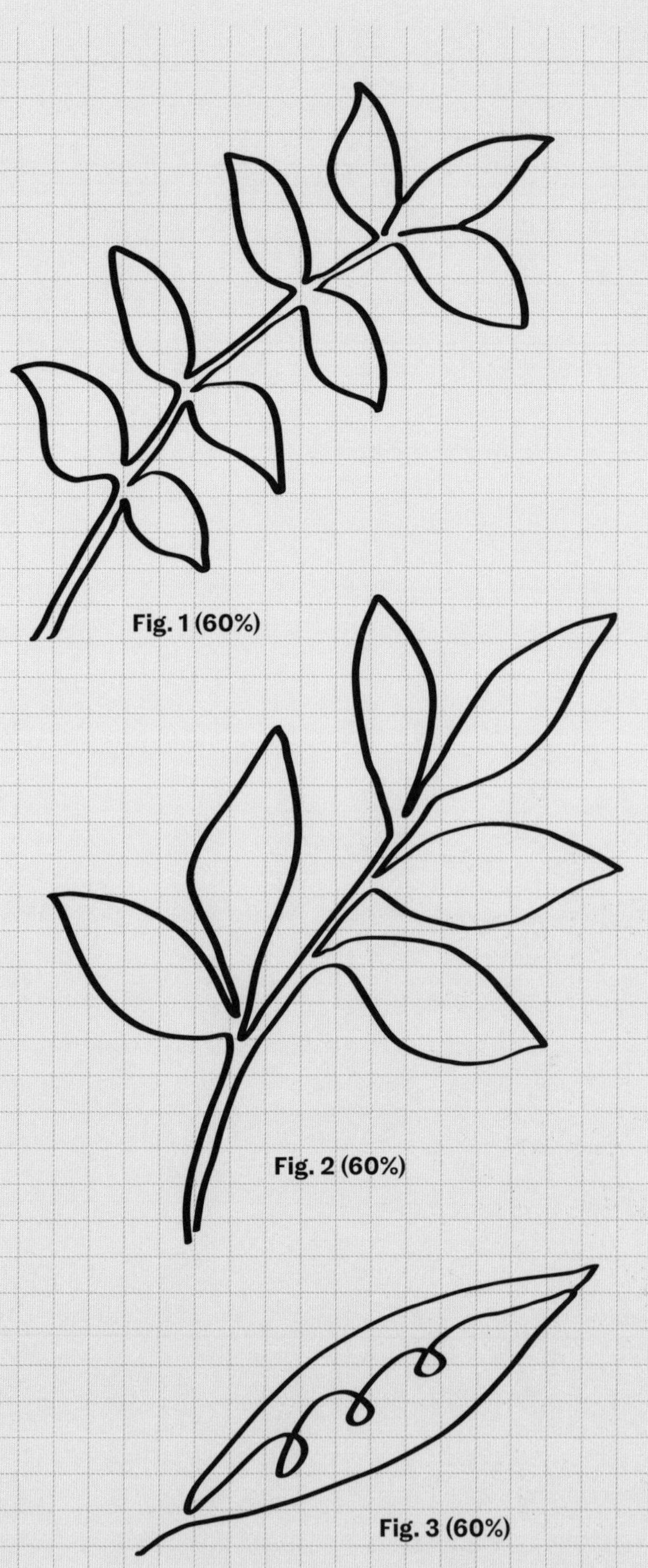

Fig. 1 (60%)

Fig. 2 (60%)

Fig. 3 (60%)

Flower Garden Jacket

This design combines my love of workwear and gardening, although you probably would not want to wear this to garden in! The shape of the jacket is a classic, simple workwear shape, made from wool cloth and unlined. I have embellished it with tulips and dahlias – my favourite garden flowers – using a combination of couched braid and appliqué. This design would work well on any jacket you want to give a new lease of life. I started with one big design on the back, then repeated elements of the design on the front pockets.

You will need

Template (see pages 148 and 149)
Scrap paper (to use for template)
Tailor's chalk or dissolvable fabric pen
Small sharp scissors
Plain wool or cotton jacket (unlined)
Dressmaking pins
Tacking (basting) thread (optional)
Embroidery needle
Small and large embroidery hoops
Base yarn: embroidery threads (floss), ribbon and Russia braid
PVA glue
Top thread: complementary sewing thread
Wool felt, for appliqué
Embroidery threads (floss) for extra filling areas

TIP

There are three different flowers on this jacket, with three different techniques. I would recommend doing a small sample of each one before you start on the jacket.

TULIPS

Here I have filled the petals of the flower with many lengths of Russia braid. For the closed tulip I used a thicker 4 mm (3/16 in) braid and for the more open tulip a 3 mm (1/8 in) braid which gives each one a slightly different finish (but both are embroidered in the same way). When you draw these flowers, make sure you work in one continuous line so that you can quickly go from start to finish with as few breaks as possible.

1. Hoop your fabric around the first flower.
2. Fix the end of the braid using glue and fold it under itself.
3. To start the tulip, lay the braid down with the folded-under end at the beginning of the design. Start at one corner of the design and work your way across it in one line without breaks if possible. Pin the braid in a few places to start with (I usually pin in sections so that my thread does not get caught on the pins). Work in close zigzags, folding the braid back on itself at the top and bottom of the petal **(Fig. 1)**.
4. Thread the needle with a double thread that matches the colour of the braid and tie a knot in the end. Come up through your fabric at the end of your braid and do a few back stitches **(see page 33)** into the folded-under end to secure it there.
5. Continue to back stitch along the centre of the braid. Once you have stitched down this first part, take the pins out and either continue pinning as you go, or just use your non-dominant thumb to guide the braid.
6. When the tulip is complete, finish the end of the braid by covering it in glue as you did at the start, fold it under itself and stitch a couple of times again to finish.

Fig. 1

Note: use this same technique to stitch both the open and closed tulips with the two different width braids. If using a thicker braid on the open tulip, just omit some of the lines in the template drawing. I have used some embroidery thread (floss) to fill in gaps around the edges of the open tulip flower to give the shape more impact. I did this using back stitch **(see page 33)**, stitched close together in rows to fill the small spaces.

FLAT-FACED DAHLIA

This dahlia, which uses appliqué, felt and embroidery thread (floss), has a more open, classic petal shape. I used wool felt as the base for the embroidery, with soft 3 mm (⅛ in) Russia braid for the centre of the flower and couched embroidery thread (floss) to add texture to the petals. I made this as a separate felt patch, creating the yellow centre first, and then used the couched lines along the petals to stitch it down to the jacket. This means the ends of the petals are loose and more three-dimensional. The flower shape is cut from wool felt, so the edges will not fray.

1. Make a template for your flower shape from paper and draw around it on your fabric with a dissolvable fabric pen. Cut out your wool felt shape with sharp fabric scissors.

2. Draw details in the centre of the petals freehand or make a stencil.

3. Thread the needle with a strong single thread and knot one end.

4. For the coil in the centre cut a 7 cm (2¾ in) length of braid and finish the ends with glue.

5. Start the coil in the centre by stitching the end on its side using stab stitch **(see page 34)**, but fold it over once at the end by about 5 mm (¼ in) while the glue is still a little wet to give it a bit of strength. Push the needle from the back of the fabric into the centre of the flower. At the same time, hold the braid on the surface of the fabric on its side and push the needle up through the fabric and the side of the braid. Do a couple of stitches here.

6. Gradually wrap the braid around the central point and do stab stitches to secure it as you go along.

7. When you come to the end of the braid, do a final couple of stitches from the end of your braid across into the braid next to it.

8. To make the wavy line on the second larger circle that surrounds the coil, follow step 7 of the pom-pom dahlia **(see page 136)**.

9. For the detail lines on the petals, I used a single strand of embroidery thread (floss), following a wide zigzag up and down each petal using basic couching stitch **(see page 32)**.

POM-POM DAHLIA

This is my version of a pom-pom dahlia and the whole flower is made up of Russia braid on its side in wavy S-shaped rows. For this flower, you will need a 4 mm (3⁄16 in) braid, and matching thread. I find the thinner braids to be much softer, making it difficult to stitch on its side, so use 4 mm (3⁄16 in) braid or larger.

1. Start by drawing out two circles, one inside the other, and a half circle at the centre. This is where your rows of braid will go, so make your circle imperfect to create a natural design.

2. Thread the needle with a single strand of sewing thread that matches the braid and tie the ends together to make this a double thread.

3. Hoop up your fabric with a small hoop.

4. Start in the centre with a small length of braid, sealing the end of your braid with glue.

5. Push the needle in from the back of your fabric at one end of the drawn line. At the same time, hold the braid on the surface of the fabric on its side, running vertically on top of the line, and push the needle up through the side of the braid 2–3 mm (1⁄8 in) from the end.

6. Pull the thread through and push the needle back down, right next to where you came out of the braid – this is stab stitch **(see page 34)**.

7. To make the wiggle, use one hand to loosely fold the braid over into an 'S' shape – if you are struggling, fold the braid onto a pin to keep it in place as this gives you a guideline for where your braid is going.

8. Start to stitch the braid in place along the drawn line, making the waves sit close together and join every point they meet at the bottom and top of each loop **(Fig. 1)**. Push the needle up through the braid as you did with your first stitch, but instead of coming back down in the same place, go over into the next-door part of the braid. Try to go through the centre of the side.

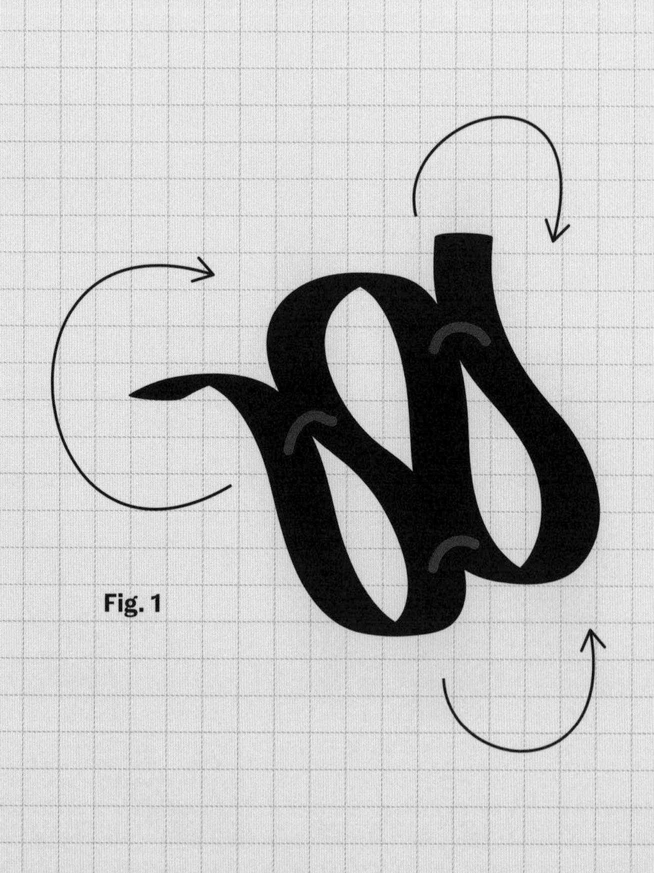

Fig. 1

9. To make the waves more open, use the single stab stitch that you used for your first stitch and make a stitch in every point that the braid curves over.
10. Continue like this along your first central part and finish it at the end with a couple of stab stitches.
11. Stitch the inner circle in the same way but with slightly larger waves, and then stitch even larger waves on the outer circle.

LEAVES

I have used alternating light green embroidered stripes on dark green fabric and dark green threads on light green wool, but you could do this in a variety of tones, or without the appliquéd material underneath.

1. Hand cut your wool in leaves of different sizes and pin to the fabric.
2. Stitch them in place around the edges using whip stitch **(see page 38)** with a matching sewing thread **(Fig. 1)**.
3. Add the decorative lines with a basic couching stitch **(see page 32)**, using a full embroidery thread (floss) as the base yarn and one thread from a darker or lighter embroidery thread (floss) to couch it down **(Fig. 1)**.
4. Hide the end of the base yarn in the fabric and stitch along the zigzag lines up and down the length of the leaves.
5. When you reach the end, hide the base yarn in the fabric and tie off at the back with a knot, or by stitching a few times into the back of the fabric.
6. To add the flower stems, cut three pieces of Russia braid of varying lengths to fit the flowers. Finish the ends with glue, turn them under and pin in place on your design. Using a double length of sewing thread, sew them down with back stitch **(see page 33)** along the centre of the braid.

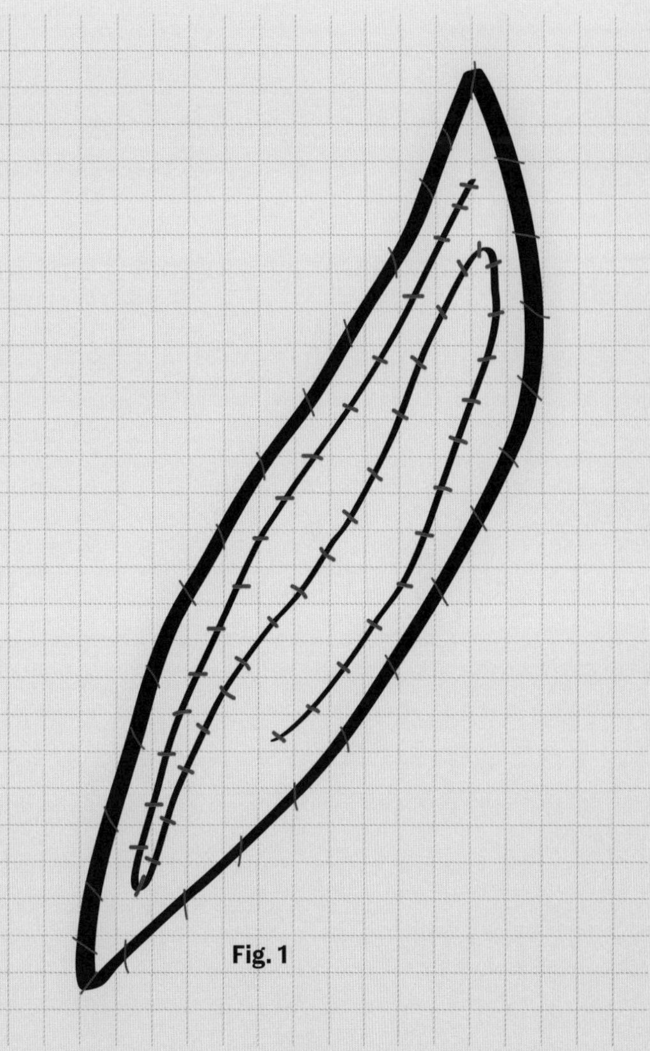

Fig. 1

Foxglove Wall Hanging

Throughout the ages wall hangings have been used to decorate homes in so many different cultures. The textures of textiles, as opposed to a picture or painting, can't be compared, especially when you use materials with contrasting qualities – here I have used vibrant and glossy silks on a dark navy linen. When choosing fabrics and threads, think about their qualities and how they will sit together. The whole piece is embroidered using waste yarn from a weaving mill. You don't have to use waste yarn, but it is a great way of recycling and works so well for couching. The same effect could be achieved with embroidery threads (floss). This design is inspired by the wild foxgloves that grow near my house. I like the simplicity of the composition, and have used short, thick strips of waste yarn to loosely replicate the looped shapes of the flowers.

You will need

Measuring tape or ruler
Linen fabric — 78 × 59 cm (30¾ × 23¼ in), which includes a seam allowance of 2 cm (¾ in) on the sides and 4 cm (1½ in) on the top and bottom
Large sharp scissors
Dressmaking pins
Tailor's chalk
Small sharp scissors
Medium embroidery hoop
Sewing machine (or you may prefer to hand sew)
Hand sewing needle
Top thread: standard machine sewing threads to match the flower yarn, stem yarn and linen background
Template (see page 150)
Base yarn: waste yarn (or long lengths of multiple threads or strips of silk fabric) in shades of green and pink
Two lengths of round 1 cm (½ in) wooden doweling — one 60 cm (24 in) piece for the top and one 52 cm (20½ in) piece for the bottom

1. Measure out the size of your wall hanging on the piece of linen and mark your cutting lines with pins or tailor's chalk (remember to add seam allowances). To find a straight line to cut down, make a little snip in the edge of the fabric where you want to start cutting, gently pull out one of the threads and cut along that line, then measure out your material using the line as a guide.

2. Fold over 1 cm (½ in) down each long side and iron the fold, then fold over again by the same amount to enclose the raw edges and iron again. You can pin across the seams every 20 cm (8 in). Sew these folded edges on your machine using a straight stitch and matching thread (stitch length 2.5).

3. For the top and bottom edges, fold over 1 cm (½ in) and iron, then fold over a wider seam of 3 cm (1¼ in). Pin and sew as in the previous step (but keep the side seams open so that the dowels can be slotted in later).

5. Mark out your design on the fabric **(see page 43)**.

6. Place the fabric in the embroidery hoop.

7. Thread the needle with a double-length of sewing thread and knot the ends together.

8. Begin by stitching the main stems, starting at the bottom and working your way up and around the leaf, and finishing with the central line of the leaf **(Fig. 1)** using basic couching stitch

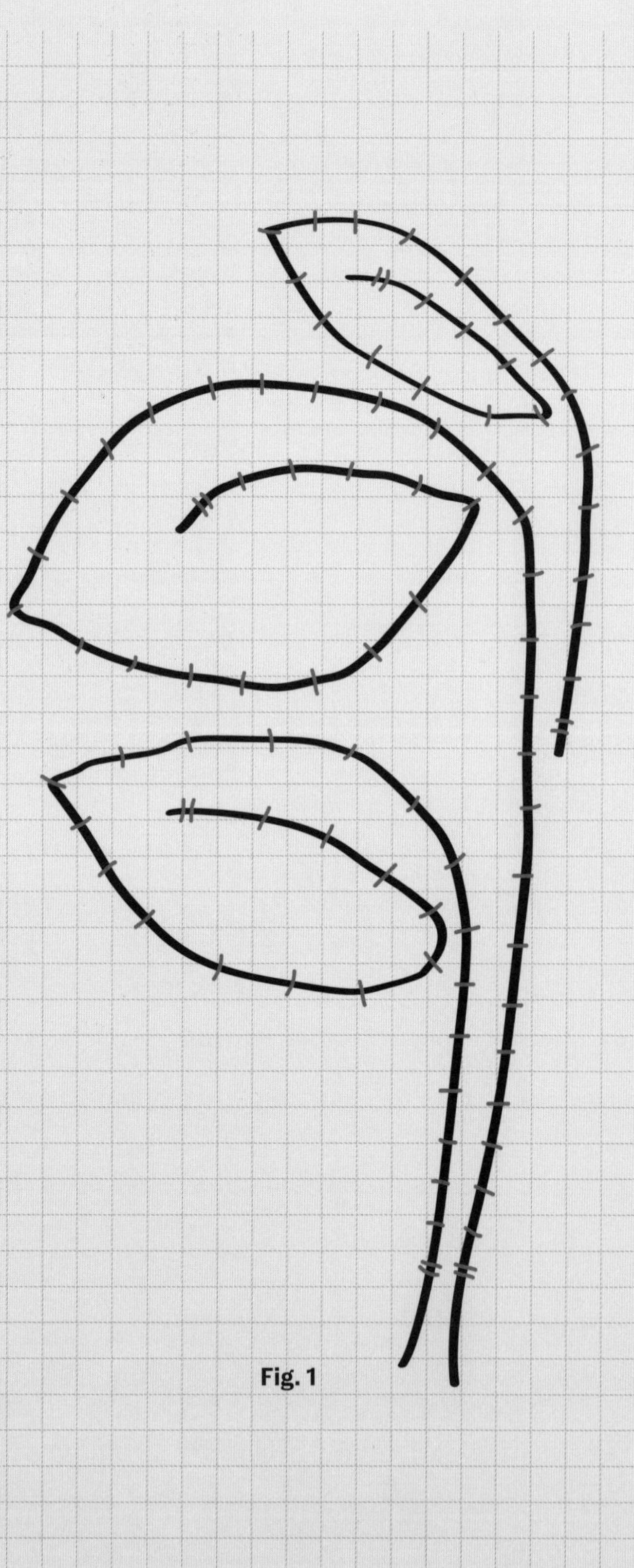

Fig. 1

(see page 32). I started each leaf at a point along the stem, which means the stem ends up being thicker due to the lines of base yarn placed next to each other. Each part of the stem then tapers off into a leaf shape. Continue with a single line of base yarn up your stem – you will cover parts of this with your flowers.

9. To stitch the flowers I used multiple strands of yarn and looped them around in a similar way to the Dandelion Brooch **(see page 70)**, but in more of a wavy zigzag shape than a figure of eight. Start with the lowest flowers and work your way up.

10. Hold the base yarn down with your non-dominant thumb and secure this end by hand stitching this first piece multiple times over the same spot until it is secure.

11. To make a loop, move your yarn into a 'U' shape following the loops in your drawing. Secure the yarn directly next to where you started, placing the stitched ends close together and letting the bottom loop hang loose **(Fig. 2)**. Stitch over the threads multiple times at the base of each of your loops to secure.

12. As you work up the stem, gradually use fewer strands of thread to make smaller flowers, using the loops to emulate the trumpet-like flowers and buds **(Fig. 3)**. Group the flowers in bunches of two and three, in varying spots along the stem, allowing some parts of the stem to be seen and some covered by flowers.

13. To make the top smallest loops, use fewer strands of thread and create smaller loops that look like buds.

14. To hang your work, slide the lengths of dowel into the channels stitched at the top and bottom of the wall hanging, with the longer piece of dowel at the top.

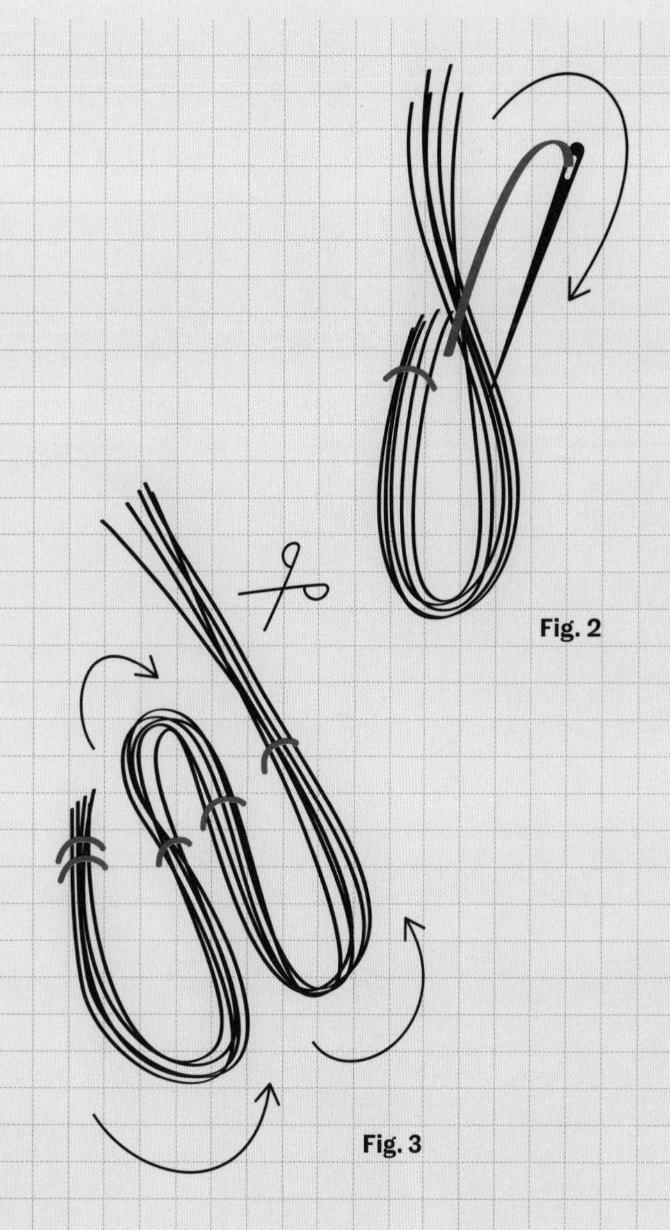

Fig. 2

Fig. 3

ROSES

Templates

BLANKET STEM (35%)
BLANKET FLOWER (35%)
BARLEY PLACEMAT (50%)

TABLE RUNNER (50%)
WAISTCOAT FRONT (50%)
WAISTCOAT REVERSE (50%)

JACKET FRONT (45%)
JACKET POCKET (45%)

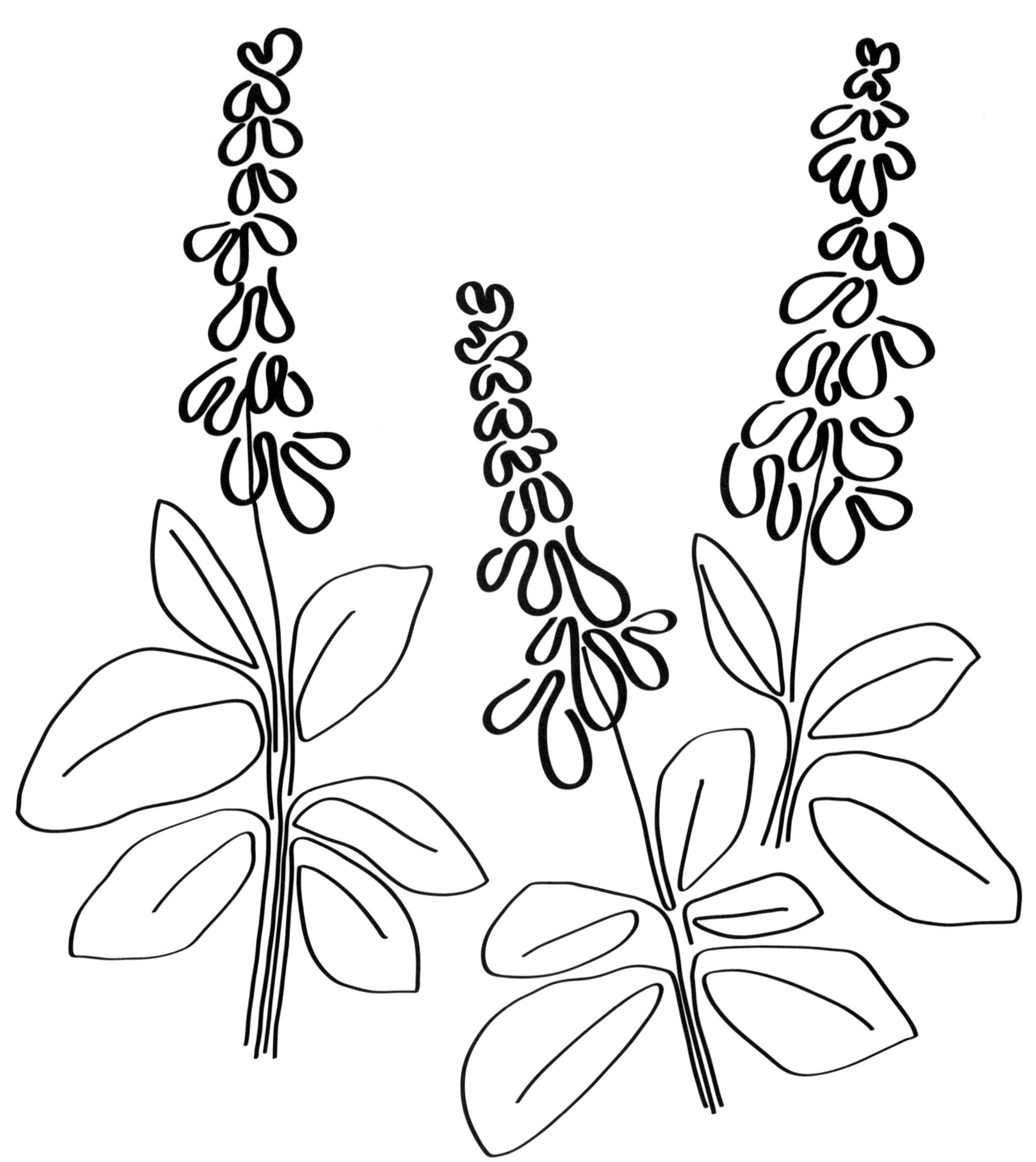

TABLE RUNNER (50%)

FERN LEAF (50%)

About The Author

Lora Avedian is a textile artist and designer from London, specialising in embroidery and embellishment. Lora has made couture textiles for interiors, arts and fashion. She sells her textiles through The New Craftsmen and Fortnum & Mason in London, as well as on her own website. She has run workshops at Barbican Centre, Royal Academy of Arts, Chateau Dumas and Leighton House Museum to name a few.

Acknowledgements

I started writing this book in the middle of a pandemic, and although it has been hard work, it really has been a saving grace for me to focus on during this extraordinary and scary time.

Thank you to the team at Hardie Grant; to Kajal Mistry for seeing potential in my work and guiding me through the process of making this book, and to Kate Burkett – it has been a pleasure to work with you both.

Thank you to Clare Newsam for your amazing design and art direction skills; you contacted me years ago about designing my identity, and I am so glad you did, it has been such a great journey working with you. I am looking forward to see what we can do next.

Thank you to Matt Russell for taking such stunning photographs and who I enjoyed working with so much. Thank you to his assistant Matthew Hague and my assistant Logan Kelly, who made things flow so much easier on the shoot days. We had such a nice team, and I really appreciate all of the hard work everyone put in to making this a beautiful book.

Thank you to the gorgeous Safia El-Dabi for making time in your very busy schedule to model for me; I am so glad you did.

A huge thank you to the ladies who run Wolves Lane Flower Company, Marianne and Camilla; they are a powerhouse. I love their ethos, what they are doing to help the environment and their community. Thank you for letting us into your world, you grow the most stunning flowers.

Thank you to my mum for sewing the waistcoat, wall hanging, curtain and cushion for me. She was the person who got me interested in textiles from a young age, and she is always there to help me whenever I need it. I am forever grateful to you for your skills and generosity with your time.

I am very pleased my daughter was able to make it in here too; thank you to her for modelling the waistcoat so beautifully – she is such a joy, and she hopefully won't look back at this with too much embarrassment. To my father and sister, thank you for your ongoing support and patience with me when I have not been able to see you because I have too much work to do.

Thank you so much to my uncle John Morris, who has helped with this process. I really appreciate you spending your time with me.

To everyone else who has supported me in one way or another along this journey, and all of the people on social media for following me. I have met so many inspiring and kind people through my platforms, and I truly appreciate the encouragement I get from everyone.

Lastly I want to say a huge thank you to my husband Erling for always being such a patient and positive influence on me. You have been so encouraging and loving throughout this process. I would not be able to follow my passion in the way I am today without you.

Resources And Suppliers

For each piece I have made a point of buying any pre-made products from small independent companies and have used second-hand or sustainably sourced materials to make the work from. I encourage you to look at these resources listed below, but to also to make a point of finding some small suppliers local to you or to use materials or garments you already have if you can.

Alex Begg & Co
Carrier Company Norfolk
Ebay
Once Milano
Rebel Rebel Flowers
Wolves Lane Flower Company

Fabrics

Cloth House
Merchant and Mills
Whaleys Fabric

Haberdashery and yarn

Barnett & Lawson
Gainsborough Weaving
Loop London
Petersham's Millinery Supplies
West Yorkshire Spinners
Wool & the Gang

Cushion:
Dandilions.

Index

Project titles are in *italics* — Page references for illustrations are in *italics*

Published in 2021 by Hardie Grant Books,
an imprint of Hardie Grant Publishing

Hardie Grant Books (London)
5th & 6th Floors
52–54 Southwark Street
London SE1 1UN

Hardie Grant Books (Melbourne)
Building 1, 658 Church Street
Richmond, Victoria 3121

hardiegrantbooks.com

British Library Cataloguing-in-Publication Data.
A catalogue record for this book is available from the British Library.

Stitch in Bloom
ISBN: 9781784883966

10 9 8 7 6 5 4 3 2 1

Publisher and Commissioner: Kajal Mistry
Project Editor: Kate Burkett
Design and Art Direction: Clare Newsam
Illustrations: Lora Avedian
Photographer: Matt Russell
Model: Safia El-Dabi
Copy-editor: Gillian Haslam
Proofreader: Sarah Herman
Indexer: Cathy Heath
Production Controller: Katie Jarvis

Colour reproduction by p2d
Printed and bound in China by Leo Paper Products Ltd.